THE THRONE

THE THRONE

1,000 YEARS OF BRITISH CORONATIONS

IAN LLOYD

DEDICATION

To my beloved and much missed mum
Irene Lloyd 1922–2022

First published 2023

The History Press
97 St George's Place, Cheltenham,
Gloucestershire, GL50 3QB
www.thehistorypress.co.uk

British Library Cataloguing in Publication Data.
A catalogue record for this book is available from the British Library.

ISBN 978 1 80399 286 0

Typesetting and origination by The History Press
Printed and bound in Great Britain by TJ Books Limited, Padstow, Cornwall.

Trees for Life

CONTENTS

FOREWORD

The main elements of the coronation of King Charles III can be traced back to Pentecost 973, when King Edgar 'convoked all the archbishops, bishops, judge and all who had rank and dignity' to assemble at Bath Abbey to witness his consecration as monarch.

There was no set venue for pre-conquest kings to hold their coronation ceremonies at. Besides Bath, they took place in London, Winchester and even Kingston upon Thames. Nine days after the consecration of Westminster Abbey on 28 December 1065, it is assumed to have been the venue for the coronation of Harold II, the last Anglo-Saxon king. This book will examine the thirty-eight ceremonies held at the abbey for the subsequent rulers, from William I to Elizabeth II (as well as the proposed coronations for the two uncrowned monarchs, Edward V and Edward VIII).

While other European countries have abandoned elaborate coronations in favour of enthronement and inauguration ceremonies, the British monarch is still crowned in a ceremony that retains many of the rites that Henry V, Elizabeth I or Queen Victoria would recognise.

The coronation has always had five main elements: the recognition and oath, the anointing, the investing, the crowning, the enthronement and homage, and the final procession.

1. The Recognition. When the monarch enters the abbey, they are taken by the archbishop to face the east, south, west and north sides of the abbey to call for recognition of the sovereign using the words: 'Sirs, I here present unto you [the monarch's name], your undoubted King/Queen. Wherefore all you who are come this day to do your homage and service, are you willing to do the same?'

2. The Oath. After the people present in the abbey acclaim the monarch, they promise to govern the UK and all their overseas territories, exercise law and justice and maintain the Protestant religion.

3. The Anointing. The monarch is then seated in the Coronation Chair and anointed by the archbishop. This was the only part of Elizabeth II's coronation not to be photographed or televised as she regarded it as a sacred moment. Holy oil is poured from an Ampulla onto the Coronation Spoon, a late twelfth-century silver-gilt spoon which was the only item of the medieval crown jewels not to have been melted down and sold off by the Parliamentarians after the English Civil War.

4. The Investing. The monarch is then robed in the *colobium sindonis* (a simple white linen shift) over which is placed the more ornate *supertunica*, a gold, silk, full-length, sleeved coat. They receive items of royal regalia including the Orb, surmounted by a cross, a ring representing the sovereign's 'marriage' to the nation, the Sceptre with Dove, and the Sceptre with Cross. The latter contains the Cullinan I (also known as the Star of Africa), the largest clear-cut diamond in the world, given as a much larger uncut gem, to Edward VII in 1907.

5. The Crowning. St Edward's Crown is brought from the High Altar and taken to the Coronation Chair by the dean, who hands it to the archbishop. After it is placed on the monarch's head, the congregation shout three times in unison: 'God Save the King/Queen.'

6. The Enthronement. The sovereign is taken from the Coronation Chair and is seated on the throne, where the statement beginning 'Stand firm, and hold fast from henceforth ...' is said. In its original Latin, the formula was first used in tenth-century English coronations.

7. Homage. The Archbishop of Canterbury and senior clergy are traditionally the first to then kneel in homage to the crowned and anointed sovereign, followed by the royal dukes and representatives of the peerage.

8. Final Procession. The monarch arrives at the abbey wearing crimson robes of state. After they retire to St Edward's Chapel, they return in procession through the abbey wearing the Imperial State Crown and a robe of purple velvet, prior to leaving through the Great West Door.

While the above format has been more or less adhered to down the centuries, everything from the accompanying music to the processions to the abbey has varied immensely.

The length of the service has grown shorter over the centuries. Elizabeth II's coronation lasted three hours, while that of the first queen regnant, Mary Tudor, ran for five hours. On the other hand, the time between accession and coronation has grown. William the Conqueror was crowned on the day he became king, for fear another claimant could snatch the throne. It was sixteen months from Elizabeth II's accession to her ceremony to give time for mourning and then preparation.

The day a coronation is held has also changed. For two-thirds of a millennium of coronations, the ceremony was held on either a Sunday or a saint's feast day, whereas the Met Office recommended 2 June for Elizabeth II as it had the highest probability of good weather (though ironically it poured down).

The procession to and from Westminster Abbey has also varied through the centuries. For 300 years, from the coronation of Richard II to that of Charles II, the monarchs traditionally processed from the Tower of London to Westminster on the eve of their coronation. The following morning, they then formed up at Westminster Hall with the clergy, nobility and the regalia before processing to the abbey for the service. This was also discontinued. Since the coronation of William IV, the monarch has instead ridden in a carriage procession – in the Gold State Coach since Victoria's coronation – down the Mall and through Whitehall. George VI and Elizabeth II both extended the return route to go back to the palace via Piccadilly Circus, Oxford Street and Park Lane to enable more people to witness the spectacle.

Developments in the media have made some of the most fundamental changes to the way the coronation is now perceived. George V allowed a photographer, Sir Benjamin Stone, to photograph certain parts of the ceremony. His son, George VI, agreed to live radio coverage of the service, and the BBC filmed a short section of the return procession as its first major outside broadcast on its fledgling television service. It was Elizabeth II's agreement, after her initial reluctance, to allow television cameras into the abbey to broadcast her coronation live that was the most radical departure. For the first time in a thousand years, the monarch was truly crowned before all her people.

Ian Lloyd
Oxford
February 2023

THE NORMANS
1066 –1154

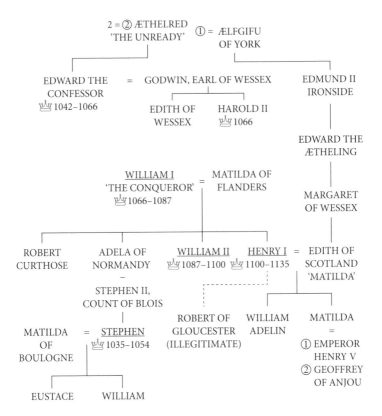

2 = ② ÆTHELRED 'THE UNREADY'   ① = ÆLFGIFU OF YORK

EDWARD THE CONFESSOR ♕ 1042–1066 = GODWIN, EARL OF WESSEX

EDMUND II IRONSIDE

EDITH OF WESSEX   HAROLD II ♕ 1066

EDWARD THE ÆTHELING

WILLIAM I 'THE CONQUEROR' ♕ 1066–1087 = MATILDA OF FLANDERS

MARGARET OF WESSEX

ROBERT CURTHOSE

ADELA OF NORMANDY – STEPHEN II, COUNT OF BLOIS

WILLIAM II ♕ 1087–1100   HENRY I ♕ 1100–1135 = EDITH OF SCOTLAND 'MATILDA'

MATILDA OF BOULOGNE = STEPHEN ♕ 1035–1054

ROBERT OF GLOUCESTER (ILLEGITIMATE)   WILLIAM ADELIN

MATILDA = ① EMPEROR HENRY V ② GEOFFREY OF ANJOU

EUSTACE   WILLIAM

WILLIAM I
1066–1087

Also known as William the Conqueror and William the Bastard, William was the illegitimate son of Robert II, Duke of Normandy, and Arlette, the daughter of a tanner. He became the ruler of Normandy in 1035 at the age of about 7, later proving a capable leader and quelling a series of rebellions. He was a contender for the throne of England following the death of the childless Edward the Confessor, defeating his main rival who had claimed the throne as Harold II at the Battle of Hastings. He spent the first decade of his reign dealing harshly with uprisings throughout his new kingdom. He consolidated his position by building some eighty castles at strategic positions, including Windsor and the White Tower (later the Tower of London). He was responsible for the Domesday Survey of England, which was published as the two-volume Domesday Book. He married Matilda of Flanders.

Coronation of William I, 25 December 1066

William's coronation was the third ceremony to be held in the newly built Westminster Abbey in a year, following the funeral of Edward the Confessor and the coronation of Harold II.

1066 was the year of three monarchs: Edward, Harold and William. It is a rare occurrence, having only happened another two times in the UK in a thousand years. In 1485 the boy-king Edward V reigned for just two months following the death of his father Edward IV and the accession of his uncle, and possible assassin, Richard III. Then again in 1936,

William the Conqueror being crowned. Pandemonium ensued when the shouts of acclamation panicked William's troops who, fearing a riot was starting, set fire to adjacent buildings as a distraction.

when Edward VIII reigned for 325 days between the death of his father George V and his own abdication, which led to the accession of his brother George VI. There is a possible fourth year. It is open to debate whether we should recognise Lady Jane Grey, the Nine Days' Queen, as ruler (she is not generally included in the list of monarchs). If we do add her name, then in 1553 there were three monarchs: Edward VI, Jane, and Mary I.

Before 1066 there was no fixed location for coronations. William may well have chosen Westminster Abbey to reinforce his claim to be the legitimate successor of the abbey's founder, Edward the Confessor, his first cousin once removed. Edward had died childless and, on his deathbed, named the English Earl Harold Godwinson as his successor. William claimed he had been promised the throne by the Confessor and invaded England in the late summer of 1066, defeating and killing Harold at the Battle of Hastings on 14 October that year.

However, the Conqueror's accession was far from a foregone conclusion. Following the battle, the Witan, the King's council made up of senior clergy and noblemen, at first backed Edgar Ætheling, the teenaged great-grandson of Æthelred the Unready. Meanwhile, William seized the southern towns of Dover, Canterbury and Winchester (the latter being the site of the Royal Treasury). At Wallingford, Archbishop Stigand of Canterbury, a senior member of the Witan, submitted to William. Shortly afterwards the claimant Edgar and senior nobles capitulated to the Conqueror at Berkhamsted.

William now needed to be crowned in order to sanctify his claim to the throne. He shrewdly devised a hybrid ceremony comprising the Anglo-Saxon rites used at the coronation of King Edgar in 973, to be performed by Archbishop Ealdred of York, and the Norman rites, which would be conducted by Geoffrey of Coutances, in French.

The kings of France were anointed with chrism, a holy oil made up of olive oil scented with sweet perfume, usually balsam. William became the first Norman king to be anointed in this way, beginning a tradition that has continued to the present day. It elevated him from Duke William the Bastard to the sanctified King of England. Another tradition that is still maintained is the reading out of the statement 'Stand firm, and hold fast from now on ...' when the monarch is brought to the throne and seated. This is a translation from the Latin prayer *Sta et retine* ..., and in William's case had to be adapted since in early medieval times it included a reference to the new monarch's father. Given the Conqueror's illegitimacy, it was thought more appropriate to change it to accession 'by hereditary right'.

The most significant addition to the English coronation ritual was the use of the *Laudes Regiae*, a hymn that had been sung at the coronation of Charlemagne as Holy Roman Emperor in AD 800, and which would have been chanted by the clergy at the 1066 ceremony.

An influence from even further afield was the new crown worn by William, which was based on a design worn by the biblical Solomon, King of Israel, and was 'fashioned out of gold and precious stones', including a sapphire, an emerald and a large central ruby.

The bilingual service led to an unexpected problem when all those present in the abbey were asked to acknowledge William as king after he was presented to them by the archbishop. According to the English chronicler Orderic Vitalis, 'all of them gladly shouted out with one voice if not in one language that they would'. The king's Norman guard outside, 'hearing the tumult of the joyful crowd in the church and the harsh accents of a foreign [i.e. English] tongue', imagined there was a riot starting and decided to torch nearby buildings, presumably as a distraction. 'The fire spread rapidly from house to house; the crowd who had been rejoicing in the church took fright and throngs of men and women of every rank and condition rushed out of the church in haste.'

News of the fire, as well as the pandemonium caused by the mass exodus of the congregation, panicked both the king and his officiates. 'Only the bishops and a few clergy and monks remained, terrified in the sanctuary, and with difficulty completed the consecration of the king who was trembling from head to foot.' Meanwhile, outside, while some of the VIP guests helped fight the flames, others, according to Orderic Vitalis, saw it as an ideal opportunity to do some looting.

The chronicler ended his account on an ominous note: 'The English, after hearing of the perpetration of such misdeeds, never again trusted the Normans who seemed to have betrayed them, but nursed their anger, and bided their time for revenge.'

William had wanted to wait until his wife, Matilda of Flanders, could be crowned alongside him, partly to honour her but more significantly to add legitimacy to his own claim since she was of English royal descent. Matilda was a great-granddaughter of King Alfred the Great, via his youngest daughter Ælfthryth of Wessex, who married Baldwin II, Margrave of Flanders.

Matilda's coronation took place on Whit Sunday, 11 May 1068, a significant date in the Christian calendar since it was when the Holy Spirit appeared before the disciples of Christ during Pentecost. It was the first staged for a queen consort in England and the first time the word 'Regina' was used to denote her status. Prior to that, the consort had been known as the king's wife or simply companion rather than queen.

Matilda's service was conducted by Ealdred, Archbishop of York, who anointed her, gave her a ring to 'marry' her to the English people and finally crowned her. The coronation was more than a symbolic gesture. It was an empowering experience that emphasised Matilda's divine appointment, as well as making it clear to all present that she shared William's power and that the English were blessed to have her as queen.

WILLIAM II
1087–1100

During his thirteen-year reign, William successfully defended England from an invasion by Malcolm III of Scotland and, in 1097, subjugated Wales. More significantly, he managed to recover Normandy from his older brother Robert Curthose, who eventually mortgaged it to him. William is perhaps best remembered for building Westminster Hall (where recent monarchs including Elizabeth II have had their lying-in-state) and for being shot in the back and killed by an arrow in the New Forest by Walter Tirel, which may have been an accident or even an assassination ordered by William's younger brother, Henry, who seized the throne as Henry I.

Coronation of William II, 26 September 1087

The coronation of William Rufus shows the vital part the ceremony had in legitimising the claim to the throne in the eyes of the Church and the people, as there were other claimants to the throne at that time.

Rufus (Latin for 'the red' – due either to his ruddy complexion or the colour of his hair in his youth) was the third son of William the Conqueror. An older brother, Richard, died in his teens, but it was the eldest surviving child, Robert Curthose, who, under normal circumstances, would have succeeded to the throne.

William had died at Rouen on 9 September 1087 while leading an expedition against the French. He bequeathed Normandy to Robert and England to William, and, as he lay dying, is said to have given his younger son a letter to take to Archbishop Lanfranc of Canterbury asking him to crown William as *Rex Anglorum* ('King of the English').

Rufus rushed to cross the Channel, accompanied by one of his father's chaplains, Richard Bloet, whom William later made chancellor as well as Bishop of Lincoln. The new king hot-footed it to Winchester to secure the Royal Treasury before meeting with Lanfranc, whose role in confirming William as king was now crucial, as William II's biographer, Frank Barlow, stated: 'The kingdom was indeed for the moment in the arch-bishop's gift. It was generally accepted that no one could become a lawful king without coronation and unction, and that the right to crown the king pertained to the arch bishop.'

Lanfranc would have taken the Conqueror's nomination of his favourite son as a directive. He would have been aware that Edward the Confessor's deathbed nomination was instrumental in Harold II claiming the throne and that William I had claimed his right to the English throne on an alleged earlier nomination by the Confessor.

The coronation was around two weeks after William's arrival back in England – long enough to summon key members of the clergy and nobility but swift enough to carry it out before Robert or his supporters could invade. According to the *Anglo-Saxon Chronicle*, Rufus's ceremony was held on Sunday 26 September, the feast day for Saints Cosmas and Damian (although Orderic Vitalis claims it was three days later, on the 29th).

William II was crowned according to Anglo-Saxon liturgy, with the king promising to protect the clergy and to rule on behalf of his people, as well as abolishing evil laws and customs. According to the *Anglo-Saxon Chronicle*, 'all the men on England to him bowed and to him oaths swore'. Like his father, he was anointed and then crowned. It is unclear which regalia was used since the Conqueror had left his crown and sceptre to the Abbey of Saint-Étienne in Caen, the Benedictine monastery he had founded in 1063. It may be that there were several sets since the Norman kings would have used them for crown-wearing ceremonies in both England and Normandy on special religious days such as Christmas.

The danger of a French invasion was ever present as the Anglo-Norman nobles who held lands in both countries objected to the division of the Conqueror's joint kingdom between Robert and William. The year after the coronation, French barons led by the Conqueror's half-brother, Odo of Bayeux, and Robert, Count of Mortain, and barons from both sides of the Channel, laid waste to lands belonging to the king. Eventually the insurrection petered out, in part because Robert failed to join them to spearhead the campaign.

HENRY I
1100–1135

Henry I is also known as Henry Beauclerc ('good scholar'); he stabilised both England and Normandy and exercised power using 'viceroys' in Normandy and trusted nobles in England to rule on his behalf whenever he was absent from either territory. He successfully saw off the challenges to his throne by his older brother Robert Curthose, whom he eventually captured at Tinchebrai in southern Normandy and held prisoner for the rest of his life. He also issued the Charter of Liberties, which undid much of the abuses of his predecessor, William II.

Henry married his daughter Matilda to Emperor Henry V of Germany and trained his only legitimate son, William Adelin, in the art of kingship. Sadly for the king, William drowned in the White Ship *maritime disaster, destroying Henry's plans for the succession. Henry summoned Matilda, by now married to Geoffrey of Anjou after the death of her first husband, and nominated her as his heir, forcing his courtiers and nobles to swear allegiance to her. Many later broke these vows amid concerns about having a female ruler.*

Coronation of Henry I, 5 August 1100

'Throne Again' the tabloid headlines would have screamed for Henry I's coronation day in 1100. For the second time in thirteen years, a younger son of William the Conqueror had hot-footed his way to Westminster Abbey to become anointed, crowned and unassailable to the supporters of arguably the rightful heir, Robert Curthose.

On his deathbed, William I had left Normandy to Robert and England to his son William Rufus, but no provision had been made for the succession after the death of the childless Rufus. The latter's end came unexpectedly during a hunting expedition in the New Forest on Thursday 2 August 1100, which was attended by his youngest brother Henry. Instead of setting off early in the morning as usual, the hunt began after lunch. William was handed a sheaf of six arrows, taking four for himself and handing two to Walter Tirel, an Anglo-Norman knight whose father-in-law, Richard fitz Gilbert, was a close ally and distant kinsman of the Conqueror. At some point Tirel and the king became separated from the others and the knight fired an arrow that, one version has it, glanced off a stag and hit the king in the chest, piercing his lungs.

As with all unexplained royal deaths, up to and including Princess Diana, conspiracy theories abound, and what may have been a simple act of God is regarded by some biographers as murder, with Henry, who benefitted by gaining the throne, as an obvious suspect. What is often overlooked is that hunting, with or without arrows, was a dangerous sport. Thirty years earlier, William and Henry's older brother Richard was also killed in the New Forest shortly after the Conquest, when his horse careered into an overhanging branch, and Robert Curthose's illegitimate son Richard was killed in a hunting accident in the same forest less than three months before Rufus's death.

At the time of William II's death, Robert Curthose was on his way back to Normandy from four years in the Holy Land participating in the First Crusade. As the first born, he had the strongest claim to be King of England, though he would need to be on English soil to defend it, so speed was of the essence for Henry to seize the newly vacated throne. He hurried to Winchester ahead of William's body, which was buried following a funeral conducted by Geoffrey of Cambrai, Prior of Winchester Abbey (William had left the see of Winchester, and many others, without a bishop in order to control its assets).

Meanwhile, Henry had taken control of the Royal Treasury, which was handily situated nearby in one of the Conqueror's castles. He also needed the acclamation of the people, or – the next best thing – the barons, who were there on site. Annoyingly for Henry, one of them – William of Breteuil – objected, citing the homage paid to Robert by some of his baronial colleagues, as well as Henry himself. The latter drew his sword, not allowing the critical Breteuil to cause 'ill foundered delay in seizing his father's sceptre before he did'. Henry had the support of the majority of the barons, including Henry de Beaumont, Earl of Warwick, and his younger sibling Robert, Count of Meulan. His claim was based on porphyrogeniture – i.e. being born to a reigning king and queen – since his birth occurred in England after Duke William of Normandy had made his own dubious claim to the throne.

On Saturday 4 August, Henry and the Beaumont brothers presumably rode hell for leather to cover the nearly 70 miles (113km) from Winchester to Westminster in a day. The royal party stayed the night at the Palace of Westminster ready for the following day's coronation.

One problem was the lack of a handy archbishop since Anselm of Canterbury was in exile in France, following a quarrel with William II, and the frail Thomas of York was based in Ripon and not up to the sort of frantic gallop Henry would have hoped for. However, although it was a well-established tradition for the Archbishop of Canterbury to crown the new monarch, it wasn't mandatory. William I had, after all, been crowned by the Archbishop of York. Henry therefore asked Bishop Maurice of London, the senior cleric in the south of England after Anselm, to conduct the service. According to historian David Crouch, the two men 'quickly agreed a deal that if the count would repudiate his brother's cynical manipulation of church vacancies, and recall Anselm, the bishop would consecrate him king'.

A swift coronation was essential to avoid giving any of the nobles, wavering in their choice of king, time to change their mind, as William of Malmesbury points out: 'So amid the universal rejoicing Henry was crowned king on 5 August, that is to say, four days after his brother's death. These acts were more carefully carried out lest the magnates should be induced to repent their choice.'

After Henry was acclaimed king by the nobles and clergy, he was anointed with the sign of the cross on his hands, breast, shoulders, elbows and twice on the head. Bishop Maurice then blessed the crown and, with a prayer, placed it on Henry's head, before giving him the coronation ring, the staff and the sceptre. After the *Te Deum* was sung, a Mass was celebrated, with Henry taking Holy Communion. With that, the coronation was over and, according to the *Anglo-Saxon Chronicle*, 'all in this country submitted to him and swore oaths and became his man'.

Henry agreed that his coronation oath should be promulgated with his royal seal attached so that 'all in this country' did indeed 'submit to him'. The people he ruled over would now know that they had a new king but also that the iniquitous policies of William II, including the oppression of the Church, was a thing of the past. Henry also wrote to Anselm to apologise for not waiting to have him officiate at the coronation, and the archbishop forgave him.

Anselm did have his own moment in the spotlight when, on 11 November 1100, he married Henry and Edith, daughter of Malcolm III of Scotland, at Westminster Abbey 'before all the nobility of the realm'. At the end of the service Edith was also crowned consort by the archbishop and took the name 'Matilda', the name of Henry's mother, perhaps to please his Norman barons. More usefully for Henry, she gave him a link to the English since she was a great-granddaughter of Edmund Ironside from the royal family of Wessex. This further united the Norman and English factions at court and boosted Henry's claim to the throne. But it was not just a political union. The chronicler William of Malmesbury claims Henry had 'long been attached' to her, while another contemporary source says she was 'not bad looking', even if, it added, she did use too much face paint.

STEPHEN
1135–1154

According to a contemporary chronicler, Stephen ruled for 'nineteen long winters in which Christ and his saints were asleep'. Both the Scots and Welsh rose against the new monarch and in 1139 Matilda, Henry I's daughter, invaded from Anjou. The English barons were divided, supporting either the king or the would-be queen. The countryside was ravaged by the civil war, which was finally resolved with a compromise just before Stephen's death.

Coronation of Stephen, 22 December 1135

If Charles II was the 'Merry Monarch', partly thanks to his overzealous sex life, Henry I's shenanigans should at least have seen him labelled 'euphoric'. He was a serial adulterer who sired at least nine sons and thirteen daughters, all of them illegitimate. Unfortunately for his dynasty, he was sadly lacking when it came to legitimate offspring, with only one son, William Adelin, and one daughter, Matilda, surviving into adulthood.

Then disaster struck on 25 November 1120 when William drowned in the *White Ship* returning from France to England. Both the crew and passengers were drunk and the vessel hit a submerged rock called Quillebœuf, a mile north-east of the village of Barfleur.

The death of the future William III left only Matilda to succeed her father, and Henry forced his courtiers to swear oaths of allegiance to his daughter at Christmas 1126. Matilda

This illustration from the Historia Anglorum *by the chronicler Matthew Paris depicts Stephen holding Faversham Abbey, which he founded and where he was buried with his wife and son Eustace.*

was an unpopular choice partly because she was female and perceived as weaker than a male heir and partly because the Anglo-Norman barons were suspicious of the ambitions of her husband, Geoffrey of Anjou.

On 1 December 1135, Henry died while hunting near Lyons-la-Forêt, having consumed 'a surfeit of lamphreys' against doctor's orders. According to one of his biographers, Ralph Davis, 'waiting for the death of Henry I must have been like waiting for the Bomb'.

There were three main contenders for the throne: Matilda; Robert of Gloucester, the king's biological son; and Stephen of Blois, the king's nephew and grandson of the Conqueror. It was a question of who could seize the opportunity before the other two. Stephen was at Boulogne when he heard the news of Henry's death and sailed for England immediately. His cause was helped by the fact that the nobles were bound by solemn oath to remain in Normandy until the king was buried: Henry's body lay at Caen until after Christmas before being interred at Reading Abbey, which he had founded.

Meanwhile, Robert of Gloucester had attempted to close the English Channel ports to Stephen, who also found the gates of Dover and Canterbury closed to him, so headed for London. He received a popular welcome in the capital, where he was patron of two of its great churches, St Martin-le-Grand and Aldgate Priory, and the citizens acclaimed him as king, which was at least a vote of confidence, even if it wasn't legally binding.

Like his predecessors, William II and Henry I, Stephen rode like a madman to Winchester to seize the Royal Treasury. He also met up with his brother Henry who, rather handily, was Bishop of Winchester. He, in turn, pulled strings to win over Roger, Bishop of Salisbury, who held the office of Justicia and was effectively the regent, controlling the government of England in the absence of the king. They then impressed on

William de Corbeil, Archbishop of Canterbury, the importance of backing Stephen's claim while the country was so unsettled.

The archbishop at first resisted, citing the 1126 oath to Matilda, but the two bishops argued that the English nobles had been coerced into this by the king and it was therefore null and void. They also brought in Hugh Bigod, later 1st Earl of Norfolk, who claimed Henry had had a change of heart on his deathbed and released the barons and clergy from their oath to support Matilda. This was disputed by eyewitnesses at Henry's deathbed, including the Archbishop of Rouen, the Bishop of Evreux and five Anglo-Norman earls, including Robert of Gloucester. The Bishop of Angers, another non-believer of Henry's eleventh-hour *volte-face*, told one of Stephen's supporters unequivocally: 'As for your statement that the king changed his mind, it is proved false by those who were present at the king's death. Neither you nor High could possibly know his last request, because neither of you were there.'

Archbishop William agreed to crown Stephen at West-minster Abbey on 22 December, which was sparsely attended as most of the court and nobility were still with Henry's body in France. Before primogeniture became the norm in England, the nomination of the king by the previous monarch and sup-ported by the archbishops of Canterbury and York, as well as the nobility, was the conventional pathway to the throne. Canterbury's anointing and crowning of Stephen was, as Ralph Davis points out, 'not just a ceremony; it was an action which was thought to have *made* Stephen king. Henceforward even his enemies could not deny that he was king,' even if they felt he was the wrong one. Matilda certainly thought so and appealed to Pope Innocent II, who rejected her claim at the Lateran Council of 1139.

Stephen's consort, Matilda of Boulogne, was heavily pregnant at the time of Stephen's dash for the throne and joined him the following spring. Her own coronation was held on 22 March 1136, during which she promised to all Englishmen 'the liberties and good laws they had enjoyed under their predecessors'.

The Empress Matilda was still intent on pursuing her own claim to the throne and, in the summer of 1139, crossed to England with Robert of Gloucester and a small army. Over the next fourteen years the two cousins fought a civil over the succession known as the Anarchy. In 1141, Stephen was captured at Lincoln and Matilda began preparations for her own coronation at Westminster Abbey. A meeting of the clergy at Winchester backed her claim to be 'Lady of the England and Normandy', but the citizens of London rose up against her when she entered the city, and the plan to replace Stephen backfired.

Instead, it was Stephen who was once again crowned and anointed. Released from captivity, he and Queen Matilda renewed their commitment to the English as well as reaffirming their legitimacy as monarch and consort at a ceremony, this time at Canterbury Cathedral on Christmas Day 1141.

THE PLANTAGENETS
1154–1399

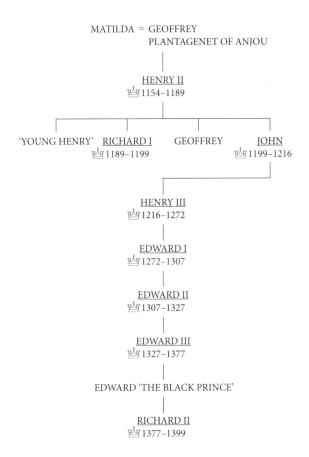

MATILDA = GEOFFREY
PLANTAGENET OF ANJOU

HENRY II
♛ 1154–1189

'YOUNG HENRY'   RICHARD I   GEOFFREY   JOHN
♛ 1189–1199   ♛ 1199–1216

HENRY III
♛ 1216–1272

EDWARD I
♛ 1272–1307

EDWARD II
♛ 1307–1327

EDWARD III
♛ 1327–1377

EDWARD 'THE BLACK PRINCE'

RICHARD II
♛ 1377–1399

HENRY II
1154–1189

Henry II expanded his Anglo-French domains and strength-ened the royal administration in England. He is remembered for his quarrels with his erstwhile friend Thomas Becket, whom he made Archbishop of Canterbury. His reign was also dogged by family conflicts between Henry, his consort Eleanor of Aquitaine and his sons, 'Young Henry', Richard the Lionheart and John Lackland.

Coronation of Henry II, 19 December 1154

Henry Plantagenet continued the efforts of his mother Matilda, daughter of Henry I, to claim the English throne, which had been occupied by Stephen of Blois since 1135. A fifteen-year civil war, known as the Anarchy, was fought by supporters loyal to either Matilda or Stephen, with neither side achiev ing victory.

Henry invaded England in 1153 and, after the second siege of Wallingford in July, met Stephen to discuss peace terms. The agreement, known as the Treaty of Wallingford, named Henry as Stephen's heir, although the latter had two sons. Conveniently for Henry, the elder son, Eustace, died the following month and his brother William showed little inclination to fight for his inheritance. The death of Eustace affected Stephen badly and he was again ready to negotiate rather than fight, and at Christmas Stephen issued a charter 'to all his liegemen of England' confirming Duke Henry as his 'son and heir'.

Stephen died on 25 October 1154, but it would be another six weeks before Henry landed in England. Having quickly taken oaths of allegiance from the barons, he prepared for his coronation alongside his wife, Eleanor of Aquitaine, on 19 December.

On the Feast of St Basil, 14 June 1170, the king's eldest surviving son, also called Henry – or 'Young Henry' – was crowned king during his father's lifetime. This was the practice of the French Capetian rulers, and it ensured the seamless inheritance of the throne from one monarch to the next. This was the only time this occurred in British history, though Stephen had tried but failed to win papal support for crowning his own son Eustace.

With Thomas Becket, Archbishop of Canterbury, in exile in France, King Henry asked Roger of Pont-l'Évêque, Archbishop of York, to conduct the service. Pope Alexander III, who had banned York from officiating, ordered Becket to lay an interdict

Henry the Young King was the only English king since the Norman Conquest to be crowned during his father's lifetime. On the right we see Henry II waiting on his son during the coronation banquet. (British Library)

on England, which meant a ban on senior clerics participating in certain rites or services in the Church. Becket also excommunicated the senior clergy who had taken part in the event. Henry was forced to negotiate with Becket at Fréteval and the latter was allowed to return to England in December 1170.

The archbishop once again infuriated Henry by announcing he would revoke the excommunication of the bishops who had taken part in Young Henry's coronation, but that only the pope could rescind the excommunication of the Archbishop of York. It was at this point that the king exploded with rage and uttered the immortal cry, 'will no one rid me of this turbulent priest', which resulted in four of his knights doing just that, murdering Becket at Canterbury Cathedral on 29 December 1170.

Young Henry went on to have an even more elaborate second coronation two years later, following his marriage to Margaret, daughter of the King of France. The service was held at Winchester on 27 August 1172, with Rotrou, Archbishop of Rouen officiating.

Young Henry didn't live to succeed his father. He died in 1183 aged 28 during a campaign against his father and his brother Richard the Lionheart. He contracted dysentery and, lying seriously ill at Martel near Limoges, he asked to be reunited with his father. The king, fearing a trick, refused to meet his son, who died on 11 June, holding a ring his father had given him in his hand. A grief-stricken Henry II is supposed to have remarked: 'He cost me much, but I wish he had lived to cost me more.'

RICHARD I
1189–1199

Richard only spent ten months of his ten-year reign in the country he ruled, while his queen, Berengaria of Navarre, never set foot in England during the time she was his consort. He regarded his kingdom as a source of revenue to fund his crusading missions. He was rumoured to have said, 'I would have sold London itself if I could have found a rich enough buyer.' He took part in the Third Crusade but on his way home he was captured by the Duke of Austria, who sold Richard to Emperor Henry VI. Richard was imprisoned by Henry for fourteen months, until his ransom was paid.

Coronation of Richard I, 3 September 1189

The first detailed record we have of a coronation is that of Richard I, thanks to the twelfth-century English chronicler Richard of Howden. Other chroniclers document the attacks, later in the day, on Jews who'd gathered to wish the new king well. This spread across the city, marring the celebrations, and would develop into widespread antisemitic rioting throughout the eastern counties of England.

The Lionheart's father, Henry II, died at Chinon, in the Loire Valley, on 6 July 1189, two days after recognising Richard as his heir in the presence of the King of France. Such a public endorsement meant there was no need for the new king to beat a hasty path to the door of Westminster Abbey to be crowned and anointed. As such, it was almost six weeks before Richard returned to England, where he was received

Archbishop Baldwin of Canterbury anoints Richard I on the head. In reality, this would have happened before the king was crowned, but this makes for a better illustration.

by his widowed mother, Eleanor of Aquitaine, at a ceremony in Winchester on 15 August. Eleanor had already deputised for her son, being present in London to receive the oaths of fealty from the Church and nobility on Richard's behalf, and she signed official documents as 'Eleanor, by the grace of God, Queen of England'.

The service was held on 3 September 1189. Howden gives us a list of participants in the procession from Westminster

Hall to the altar of the abbey along a path made of woollen cloth. We hear that John Marshal was 'carrying in his hands two large and heavy spurs from the King's treasure'. Next to him was Godfrey de Luci carrying the royal cope. 'William Marshal was carrying the royal sceptre, on the top of which was a golden cross; William earl of Salisbury was carrying the royal rod, which had a dove on top.'

Next in the procession were three earls carrying ceremonial swords in golden sheaths: Robert, Earl of Leicester, David, Earl of Huntingdon (brother of the King of Scotland), and the king's brother and eventual successor, John.

William de Mandeville, Count of Aumale, carried the heavy gold crown. Immediately behind him came Richard, walking under a silk canopy, flanked by the bishops of Bath and Durham.

At the High Altar, Richard made the oath to 'bear peace and honour and reverence' to God, the Church and its ministers, to 'administer fair justice to the people' and to destroy bad laws and uphold good ones.

At this point Richard was stripped of his outer garments down to a silk shirt that was unstitched at the shoulder and his breeches. He also took off his woven gold sandals, before being given the sceptre in his right hand and the royal rod in his left. Baldwin of Forde, Archbishop of Canterbury, anointed the king on head, shoulders and right arm. (These became the usual parts of the body for unction until the coronation of Victoria, who was only anointed on the head and hands).

After being dressed in his coronation robes, Richard broke with tradition, taking the crown from the altar and handing it to the archbishop to place it on his head. At this point, legend has it, there was an ill omen, when a bat flew in and flittered around the throne, despite it being the middle of the day.

After celebrating Mass, the king changed into a lighter set of clothes as well as a lighter crown before processing back to Westminster Hall. Here he 'feasted magnificently' on food cooked by the citizens of Winchester who manned the kitchen, serving 1,770 pitchers, 900 cups and 5,050 dishes. It was the start of three days of festivities marking the coronation.

It was as the banquet was coming to an end that things went seriously awry. A group of Jews arrived at the hall intent on presenting Richard with gifts to mark his coronation. A crowd of Christians at the gate wouldn't allow them in and a fight broke out. The disturbance spread to the city throughout the night, with some Jews killed, while others had their houses burnt down and fled to the Tower of London for protection. The king, hearing of the disturbance, was furious because the Jews were under his special protection partly because, since the Conqueror's arrival, the Norman kings had used Jewish merchants to provide them with much-needed cash to bolster their position in England.

During the following months, antisemitic riots spread north-eastwards to Lynn, Norwich, Lincoln and Stamford. The attacks reached a climax in March 1190 in York, when 150 Jews fled from attackers and sought sanctuary in the castle. As the mob grew more frenzied, many resorted to suicide, having first killed their wives and children. Those who survived and were told they would be spared if they accepted baptism into the Christian faith emerged from the castle and were promptly massacred.

A month after the York massacre, Richard sailed from Dartmouth to join Philip II of France on the Third Crusade. On his return to England in 1194, he was crowned a second time, which was a common practice for medieval kings at significant times in their reign, for instance when they married. The ceremony didn't involve unction but the Archbishop of Canterbury once again placed the weighty St Edward's Crown on the king's head, just to remind his subjects he might not always be with them in England but he was still their head of state.

JOHN
1199–1216

Immortalised by film and TV versions of the Robin Hood legend as 'the wicked king', as opposed to his older brother Richard's 'good king', John was the fourth son of Henry II. He was nicknamed 'Lackland' since his father had divided his territories between his three older sons but failed to leave anything for John. When he did inherit the throne, he lived up to his name by losing Normandy to the King of France in 1204. This, plus extortionate taxes inflicted on his subjects, eventually led to the Church and nobility forcing him to sign Magna Carta to guarantee the rights of the clergy, the barons and all his subjects.

Coronation of John, 27 May 1199

Few medieval monarchs seem to have made it to the throne without an unseemly dash across the English Channel to outwit a popular rival. John's was a more leisurely progress, but, like William II and Stephen, he was in France when his predecessor, also on French soil, inconveniently died. John also had the misfortune to be staying with his nephew, Arthur of Brittany, the other main claimant to the throne when Richard I expired.

Given his reputation as a formidable warrior and military leader, Richard Cœur de Lion died as a result of a singularly unimpressive soldierly tactic. Contemporary chroniclers claim that during the winter of 1198–99 a ploughman at Châlus, some 22 miles (36km) south-west of Limoges, unearthed a Gallo-Roman hoard. Richard, as landlord of the estate, claimed a right to the treasure trove. He decided to lay siege to the castle of Châlus-Chabrol, which he found poorly defended and no particular challenge as a target. The 41-year-old king was so relaxed about the attack that, when he set out to reconnoitre the site with his mercenary captain, Mercardier, he failed to wear full armour.

Richard was struck in the shoulder by a bolt from a crossbow, fired by a boy and one of only two people defending the castle. The wound turned gangrenous and the king died ten days later, on 6 April 1199, in the arms of his mother, Eleanor of Aquitaine. Given various identities by the chroniclers, with Pierre Basile as the favourite, the bowman was brought before the dying monarch. Expecting to be executed for his action, instead 'Basile' was forgiven and sent home with 100s as a bonus. (At least one account has him skinned alive by Mercardier, which is more likely.) The castle didn't fare as well: Richard asked for his body to be buried at Fontevraud, at the foot of his father's tomb, and his heart to be sent to Notre-Dame Cathedral in Rouen, but instructed that Châlus should receive his entrails.

On his deathbed, Richard bequeathed his jewels to his nephew Otto of Saxony and his throne to his younger brother John. With primogeniture still not the clear rule, it helped the latter's cause that he had the late king's endorsement. He promptly set off to Chinon to lay claim to the Plantagenet rulers' Angevin treasury, just as his great-grandfather Henry I had hurried to Winchester to seize the English treasury before his older brother Robert had the opportunity.

Yet the succession was far from clear cut. Contemporary chroniclers reflected the popular mood by backing either John or 12-year-old Arthur, the son of John and Richard's late brother Geoffrey II, Duke of Brittany. 'In the circumstances of a contested succession,' writes John's biographer W.L. Warren, 'acceptance by a sufficient number of influential men to secure investiture was what really mattered.'

Two of the most influential figures of the time happened to be in France at the time. William Marshal, an Anglo-Norman statesman who had served both Henry II and Richard I, backed John's claim. The near-contemporary *Histoire de Guillaume le Maréchal* ('History of William the Marshal'), composed in the 1220s, tells us that news of the Lionheart's death was broken to him at bedtime when he was staying at Vaudreuil. He immediately rushed to see Hubert Walter, Archbishop of Canterbury, telling him: 'My lord we must lose no time in choosing someone to be king.' Walter backed Arthur, but Marshal felt Arthur knew nothing of England and wouldn't be committed to ruling the country. He insisted, 'a son has a better claim to his father's land than a grandson.' The archbishop reluctantly agreed, though not before warning the loyal courtier that he might live to regret backing Richard's brother.

John, meanwhile, had narrowly avoided confrontation with an army of Arthur's Breton followers raised by the prince's protector, King Philip II of France. He headed for Normandy, where the Norman barons didn't want a Breton ruler, and proclaimed John Duke of Normandy on 25 April with a coronet of golden roses.

By then the archbishop and Marshal had returned to England, where they persuaded Geoffrey Fitz Peter, the Chief Justiciar, to agree to John's succession. They also convened a meeting of barons at Northampton for the same purpose.

John landed at Shoreham on 25 May and was crowned by Hubert Walter two days later at Westminster Abbey on Ascension Day. What little information we have about the ceremony suggests the new monarch failed to treat it with gravitas, displaying 'unseemly levity' and leaving before receiving the Sacrament.

Presumably the archbishop's sermon wasn't to his liking. According to the chronicler Roger of Wendover, Hubert Walter proclaimed, 'be it known that no one has an antecedent right to succeed another in the kingdom, unless he shall have been unanimously elected under the guidance of the Holy Spirit.' He also declared that if anyone else had a greater claim 'in merit' he should become ruler instead. Asked a few years later why he had said it, the archbishop replied that 'he knew John would one day or other bring the kingdom to great confusion, wherefore he determined that he should owe his elevation to election and not to hereditary right'.

John's father Henry II had pushed for the canonisation of Edward the Confessor by Pope Alexander III in 1161, but John failed to show the same veneration for either the abbey or its founder. The next day he did, however, go to St Albans to pray at the abbey built on the site of execution of St Alban, Britain's first Christian martyr, by Roman soldiers.

Backing for Arthur would rumble on for another four years, with Philip II recognising the young prince's claim in the Treaty of Le Goulet in May 1200. In the same year, Arthur was seized by John's army and imprisoned at Falaise Castle in Normandy. John visited his nephew in 1203, asking him to back his claim. The proud prince, now aged 16 and still allied with Philip II, refused, and, like the Princes in the Tower 300 years later, he disappeared from public view and, like them, rumour has it was murdered, probably on John's orders. The Welsh *Annales de Margan* even suggests, 'When John was drunk and possessed by the devil, he slew [Arthur] with his own hand and tying a heavy stone to the body, cast it into the Seine.'

HENRY III
1216–1272

Henry was crowned twice: first aged 9, to beat a rival to the throne; and, second, three and a half years later at Westminster Abbey, to strengthen his claim as the legitimate sovereign. His reign saw recurrent struggles with the English barons trying to protect their rights enshrined in the Magna Carta, signed by his father King John in 1215. He also led two failed campaigns in France. On a positive note, he began the rebuilding of Westminster Abbey, where he was buried in a tomb near to that of his idol Edward the Confessor.

Coronations of Henry III, 28 October 1216 and 17 May 1220

King John had been 'brought down by a grave and incurable illness' and died at Newark on 18 or 19 October 1216. This was halfway through the First Barons' War in which rebellious landowners waged war against the Crown and had forced the king to sign Magna Carta at Runnymede the previous year.

John continued to refuse the terms of the charter and his uncompromising attitude led some of the barons to turn to Prince Louis, eldest son of the King Philip II of France, to replace John as king. Louis not only had baronial support, but he also had a link to the English throne via his wife, Blanche of Castile, the granddaughter of Henry II and Eleanor of Aquitaine.

Louis landed at Thanet on 21 May 1216 and initially drew support from the rebellious barons until the death of John saw many of them desert him in favour of the 9-year-old Henry.

The coronation of Henry III from a thirteenth-century manuscript illustration by Roger de Pont L'Évêque.

On his deathbed, John had tried to strengthen his son's claim by begging Pope Honorius III to take Henry under his protection, and so it was that the papal legate, Cardinal Guala Bicchieri, oversaw Henry's coronation, which was rapidly arranged for 28 October 1216. Westminster Abbey was under the control of Louis's supporters and Stephen Langton, Archbishop of Canterbury, banished from England by the pope for supporting the dissident barons. This meant that the ceremony had to take place at Gloucester Abbey with Peter des Roches, Bishop of Winchester, officiating. It is unclear if the crown had been sold off to raise money for the ongoing civil war or was lost with other jewels when the king's baggage train was trapped by rising tides in the Wash estuary between Norfolk and Lincolnshire. Instead, Henry was crowned with a simple gold circlet belonging to his mother, Queen Isabella.

Having been crowned by the wrong cleric in the wrong place, Henry was given a second coronation in May 1220 to strengthen his position as ruler now that the Barons' War was over and his enemies defeated. Langton was allowed to officiate by the pope and the ceremony took place on the Feast of Pentecost. A newly made gold crown studded with a variety of gems was used, with a gold sceptre and a silver gilt staff. Henry wore a red silk dalmatic – a wide-sleeved liturgical vestment.

At the age of 28, Henry married the 12-year-old Eleanor of Provence in January 1236 at Canterbury and, according to her biographer Margaret Howell, would almost certainly have consummated it to validate their marriage. Six days later, Eleanor was crowned queen regnant at Westminster Abbey with Henry in attendance wearing his full coronation regalia.

The chronicler Matthew Paris records that London was *en fête*, with the streets packed with onlookers, the houses draped with hangings and flags, and the winter's scene illuminated with lamps and candles. The king's trumpeter led the procession on horseback, followed by wealthy London citizens on richly caparisoned horses, carrying 360 gold and silver cups to serve the guests at the banquet after the ceremony.

Henry and Eleanor walked on blue ray-cloth from Westminster Hall to the abbey, each of them under silk canopies carried by barons from the Cinque Ports. Eleanor wore her hair loose, as was customary for a queen consort, fixed into place with a gold circlet. At the church door the archbishop recited a list of biblical women who had been blessed in bearing sons in the line of King David, culminating in the Virgin Mary. It seems to have worked as the couple went on to have five sons and three daughters.

After her anointing with holy oil, Eleanor was crowned with a heavy gold crown of lilies. Subsequently the king and queen dined on venison and fish, swilled down with wine, and were entertained by minstrels and other musicians – an altogether heady experience for a 12-year-old.

According to Matthew Paris, in 1245 Henry:

> inspired by his devotion to St Edward, ordered the church of St Peter at Westminster to be enlarged. And with the walls on the eastern side and the tower pulled down, he ordered that new, namely more fitting ones, be constructed at his own expense … and that they be joined to the remainder of the building namely at the west.

With Henry as sole patron, the masons rebuilt the abbey in the High Gothic, northern France style. Henry venerated Edward the Confessor, naming his eldest son after the abbey's founder. He erected a new and costly shrine in his honour and on 13 December 1269, together with his brother Richard, Earl of Cornwall, and his two sons, they bore the coffin of St Edward on their shoulders into its new resting place.

EDWARD I
1272–1307

Edward I, also known as Edward Longshanks and the Hammer of the Scots, was born in 1239, the eldest son of Henry III and Eleanor of Provence. He spent much of his reign in military campaigns against Wales, Scotland and France. His lasting legacy is the seventeen castles he had built in Wales, of which four of them – Beaumaris, Caernarfon, Conwy and Harlech – are now designated World Heritage Sites. He is also remembered for the twelve lavishly decorated crosses – most famously, the Charing Cross – erected in memory of his wife, Eleanor of Castile. Each cross marks the nightly resting place of her remains as her body was transported back to London following her death in 1290.

Coronation of Edward I, 19 August 1274

Whilst many of his predecessors made an undignified scramble for what Princess Diana referred to as 'the top job', becoming hailed, crowned and anointed within days of seizing the throne, it took Edward I two years to make it to Westminster Abbey.

Edward had left England in August 1270 to take part in the Ninth Crusade, under the leadership of King Louis IX of France. After sixteen months in the Holy Land, Edward left Acre for Sicily, where he was told that his father, Henry III, had died on 16 November 1272. Given that England was politically stable at the time, Edward decided against returning immediately and, having been proclaimed king *in absentia* rather than at his coronation, he took a leisurely twenty-one months to appear before his people.

The delay meant that the City of London and Edward's court had months rather than days to prepare for the coronation. The Palace of Westminster was transformed into a village ahead of Edward's return, with £1,100 spent on redecoration and temporary accommodation, stables and kitchens to cope with the thousands of expected guests. The king wanted a two-week extravaganza based on King Solomon's fourteen-day Feast of Dedication of the Holy Temple. His aim, according to a contemporary chronicler, was to create the ultimate open house 'so that all men, poor and rich, coming to the ceremony, might be freely received, and nobody sent away'.

Feeding this multitude was a logistical nightmare, with the sheriffs of twelve counties roped in to supply provisions from as early as February 1274. Gloucestershire alone sent 60 oxen and cows, 60 swine, 2 fat boars, 40 bacon pigs and 3,000 of the 22,460 capons and hens needed. Meanwhile, bishops, abbots and priors were asked to send swans, peacocks, rabbits and kids.

Edward and his queen, Eleanor of Castile, who had married in her native country when he was 15 and she two years younger, set foot on English soil at Dover on 2 August. Again, they were in no rush to enter the capital until all preparations were made for their state arrival. Instead, they took sixteen days to reach London, stopping over with baronial friends at Canterbury, Tonbridge and Reigate.

When 35-year-old Edward did reach the city, he must have been an imposing presence on horseback at 6ft 2in (188cm) tall, broad chested, dark haired and with his famously lengthy legs (which resulted in his nickname 'longshanks'). Only a drooped left eyelid – a family trait inherited from Henry III – marred his good looks.

The Tower of London had been cleaned up by the king's ministers and the refuse was removed from the normally bustling market area of Cheapside, ahead of the royal procession later in the day. The mayor had already ordered silks and cloth of gold banners to be hung 'without consideration for cost', and the conduits to flow with red and white wine, which ensured a good, loyal gathering along the route.

The ceremonial parade to Westminster gave birth to a custom that lasted until the coronation of Charles II. Another ritual was to spend the night at the Palace of Westminster, where Edward slept in the Painted Chamber in which his father died. The room was named after the painting of Edward the Confessor surrounded by clergy at his coronation. It was commissioned by Henry III during a redecoration following the fire of 1263 and, knowing that his son would spend the night before his own ceremony in prayer and contemplation in the same room, it may have been an inspired theme.

The following morning Edward and Eleanor walked from Westminster Hall to the abbey along a carpet of cloth made by the weavers of Candlewick Street (now Cannon Street) and below silk canopies hung with silver bells.

Edward was the first monarch to be crowned in the abbey since Henry III rebuilt the Confessor's original building. Work commenced in 1245 and, by the time of its consecration, attended by Edward and Eleanor in October 1269, it resembled the building we see today. Influenced by French cathedral architecture, north and south transepts were added and the nave was extended. The crossing, where the four arms of the cruciform layout meet, was made wide enough to function as the coronation theatre. An arched wooden structure, high enough for some of the baronial guests to ride their horses under, supported the throne used for the crowning by the Archbishop of Canterbury, Robert Kilwardby.

The chief guests were Prince Henry, the heir apparent, wearing a chaplet of flowers, and King Edward's sisters and their husbands: Margaret, married to Alexander III of Scotland, and

Beatrice, wife of John II, Duke of Brittany. Sadly, all three of these relatives died within months of each other – Prince Henry died two months later, aged 6, and his aunts, 'women of great fame and in the flower of their youth', the following spring.

They would have all seen Edward being anointed as king, standing on the new 25ft (7.5m) square Cosmati pavement, a multicoloured mosaic pavement, covered in rich cloth for the day, which was made in 1268 and restored most recently in 2010. They would have also witnessed the newly crowned monarch dramatically take off his gold crown and, according to a chronicler, announce 'he would never take it up again until he had recovered the lands given away by his father to the earls, barons and knights of England, and to aliens'. Historian Marc Morris thinks that, rather than returning the actual estates gifted by King Henry, he may have meant the rights that went with them in an attempt to regain some of the monarch's personal authority.

While St Edward's Crown was cast aside, Edward did don another gold crown, studded with emeralds, sapphires, rubies and pearls, for the banquet in Westminster Hall, where he and Eleanor sat, in their coronation robes, on specially made stone thrones for the banquet.

Legend has it there was another dramatic moment when, during the banquet, Alexander III and a hundred of his knights rode in on horseback, released their steeds and offered them to anyone who could catch them. At this point English knights, including Edward's brother Edmund, not to be outdone, made a similar gesture with even more horses. If, indeed, Westminster Hall was turned into a stampeding rodeo, or whether it was the result of a chronicler's overactive imagination, we'll never know.

EDWARD II
1307–1327

Edward II's coronation stands out in history for the embarrassing behaviour of his favourite, Piers Gaveston, who undoubtedly stole the show for all the wrong reasons. It was also the first time the Coronation Chair was in place, which itself would be a feature of subsequent coronations, including that of Charles III.

Edward's twenty-year reign saw constant struggles with rebellious English barons who felt excluded from power. Large debts, many of them inherited, accrued and the Scots' victory at the Battle of Bannockburn also increase his unpopularity. In 1327 he was forced to renounce the throne in favour of his son Edward, becoming the first anointed English king to be dethroned since Æthelred in 1013.

Coronation of Edward II, 25 February 1308

Piers Gaveston was the son of a Gascon knight who, through his wife's territories in Aquitaine, was a vassal of King Edward I. The king assigned him to join the household of his heir, Edward of Caernarfon. Edward junior clearly became obsessed with the young courtier and his alarmed father had Gaveston sent abroad. He returned from exile following the death of the old king and the accession of his royal friend as Edward II. The latter made Gaveston regent at the beginning of 1308, when 23-year-old Edward journeyed to France to marry King Philip II's daughter Isabella, aged 16, at Boulogne on 25 January.

The newlyweds returned to England, landing at Dover on 7 February. Gaveston was there to meet them and the besotted

The bromance between Edward II and his favourite Piers Gaveston upset courtiers, clergy and nobility, as is evident in this later depiction by Marcus Stone.

king ran to him and fell into his arms 'giving him kisses and repeated embraces' and calling him 'brother', much to the horror of Isabella, who stared at them in disbelief.

The coronation, originally scheduled for the 18th of the month, was postponed for a week, mainly because many of the barons threatened not to take their oaths of allegiance unless Gaveston was banned from the ceremony. Isabella's two uncles, who had accompanied her to England, also vowed to boycott the ceremony out of loyalty to the young queen.

At a pre-coronation banquet at Eltham Palace, Gaveston, 'whose passion for finery was insatiable', unbelievably wore some of the jewels that Isabella had brought with her from France as part of her dowry. Unsurprisingly, the bride of three weeks wrote to her father to tell him that she was 'the most wretched of wives'.

In order to placate them all, Edward promised the nobles concessions 'to undertake whatever they sought in the next parliament', which was due to meet in March. His opponents acquiesced and Gaveston retained his place in the proceedings.

On 19 February, Edward and Isabella made their ceremonial entrance in to London in a 4-mile procession through the city, where the usual conduits of wine, flag-draped buildings and cheering throngs made it a memorable event. They stayed five nights at the Tower of London before processing to Westminster.

On the 25th, the couple walked from the Palace of Westminster to the abbey on a raised timber walkway covered in blue cloth and strewn with flowers and herbs. The crowds were so thick that they were obliged to enter the sacred building through a back entrance.

Despite the ongoing baronial opposition to him, Gaveston was still in charge of the coronation preparations, giving himself a plum role in every aspect of the proceedings. According to the chronicler Robert of Reading, he appeared in the arrival procession 'so decked out that he more resembled the god Mars than an ordinary mortal'. He wore a pearl-encrusted robe that, against all protocol, was in the purple colour associated with royalty, whereas his fellow peers wore the usual cloth of gold. Gaveston also carried in the crown of St Edward the Confessor, a role traditionally reserved for the more senior peers. The contemporary author of the *Annales Paulini* recalled that one peer was so incensed he very nearly came to blows with Gaveston during the ceremony.

In the absence of Archbishop Winchelsey of Canterbury, the service was conducted by Henry Woodlock, Bishop of Winchester. For the first time, the king took the oath in French rather than Latin, perhaps to make it easier for the overwhelmingly French-speaking congregation. It was also the first coronation that peers' wives were allowed to attend, in honour of the queen.

The most striking innovation was the use of the new Coronation Chair elevated on a wooden dais before the High

Altar. It was made by order of Edward I and designed to hold the Scone of Scone, which he had seized from Scotland in 1296. The oak chair was made by the craftsman and painter Walter of Durham, who decorated it with patterns of birds, foliage and animals on a gilt background. The 6ft 9in-high (2.05m) chair has had an eventful history. It was taken across to Westminster Hall for Oliver Cromwell to sit on when he was created Lord Protector during the Interregnum. During less

The coronation of Edward II was the first time the Coronation Chair, made for Edward I, featured in the ceremony. There was such a melee inside the abbey that a section of wall collapsed, killing a knight.

reverential times, it was defaced by generations of Westminster schoolboys, one of whom carved 'P. Abbott slept in this chair 5–6 July 1800' on the seat. In 1914 a bomb, thought to have been placed by suffragettes, blew a corner of the chair off and, to protect it from enemy bombing in the Second World War, it was evacuated to Gloucester Cathedral. In 1950 Scottish nationalists broke into the abbey and stole the Stone of Scone, though it was found and returned in time for the coronation of Elizabeth II in 1953.

After Edward was crowned and the congregation paid homage, Isabella was then anointed – though only on the hands – before being crowned with a gold circlet studded with jewels.

Gaveston's lack of expertise as an events manager is evident from two incidents from the ceremony. Firstly, there were so many spectators allowed in that the crowds were almost crushing the king and clergy during the moment of crowning. More alarmingly, such was the jostling of bodies that a section of wall behind the High Altar collapsed, killing one knight.

Nor did things get any better back at Westminster Hall for the traditional banquet. The newly crowned king and queen arrived back at 3 p.m. but the timings were so badly messed up that it was dark by the time they tucked into the food, which was largely inedible despite having been brought in from suppliers throughout the southern counties, along with wine from Gascony.

By now the royal *ménage à trois* had noticeably become a *ménage à deux*, as the king ignored his young consort and visibly flirted with Gaveston. The nobles and the French uncles seethed with rage at the display from the king's table, as well as at the tapestries decorating the hall that combined the arms of Gaveston's dukedom of Cornwall with those of the king, with Isabella's heraldic emblems hanging forlornly to one side.

Karma prevailed, even if Gaveston did not. Edward had no alternative but to exile him four months later and, following his return, he was condemned to death in 1312. Edward also met a sticky end fifteen years later, when Isabella and her lover Roger Mortimer orchestrated the king's downfall. It is still unclear how Edward met his end at Berkeley Castle on 21 September 1327. One persistent myth, loved by generations of schoolchildren, is that, in a reference to his romance with Piers Gaveston, he may have been murdered by having a red-hot poker shoved where the sun don't shine.

EDWARD III
1327–1377

Edward III is the sixth-longest-reigning monarch in British history, having ruled for 50 years and 147 days. He was born at Windsor Castle on 13 November 1312 and was also known as Edward of Windsor. In 1348 he founded the Order of the Garter, the country's oldest order of chivalry. The discovery of the foundation trench of a circular building some 200ft (61m) in diameter in the Upper Ward of the castle, which Edward had ordered to be constructed in 1344 (though it was never completed), suggests he may have been trying to emulate the idea of an Arthurian 'knights of the round table'.

His reign saw the beginning of the Hundred Years War against France, which started with significant victories for the English at the battles of Crécy and Poitiers. This led to Edward securing huge territorial gains, giving him control of a quarter of France, following the Treaty of Brétigny. Having transformed England into a formidable fighting power, the final part of his reign witnessed a complete change of fortune. As the tide of victory turned against him, the French king, Charles V, managed to reverse many of the English conquests under the 1375 Treaty of Bruges. The huge costs of the war and the military defeats proved unpopular in England, where high taxes and the devastating effect of the 1348 Black Death epidemic had adversely affected the economy. In 1376 the Good Parliament refused to grant the king the necessary funds to continue the war.

By then Edward was failing in health and desperately sad at the death of his heir, Edward, the Black Prince. He died on 21 June 1377 and was succeeded by his 10-year-old grandson, Richard II.

Coronation of Edward III, 1 February 1327

Edward III was a pawn, first of all in the hands of his father, Edward II, who used his young son to deputise for him, and then later under the thumb of his mother. Isabella of France and her lover, Roger Mortimer, gained control (as well as substantial revenue) by seizing England in the name of her teenaged son.

Edward II proved an ineffectual and unpopular leader. His father may have been 'the Hammer of the Scots', but the younger Edward couldn't even manage a light tap. In the summer of 1314, he was at the head of the largest army to ever invade Scotland – 25,000 infantry and 2,000 horses – against an enemy army of only 6,000 men, and they were thoroughly trounced. The Battle of Bannockburn on 23–24 June proved a landmark moment in Scottish history, eventually forcing England to accept full Scottish independence and the right of Robert the Bruce and his successors as monarchs.

Edward was always ruled by his heart rather than his head and, despite his marriage to Isabella of France and fathering four legitimate children as well as an illegitimate son, Adam

In 1348 Edward III founded the Order of the Garter, the country's oldest order of chivalry. This illuminated manuscript in the Garter Book, commissioned by William Bruges, shows the king on the left in his garter robes. (The History Collection/Alamy Stock Photo)

FitzRoy, the king had a succession of male lovers. He gave them all too much power and influence, ending up with them alienating the nobility, Church and the people.

Tension between the last favourite, Hugh Despenser, and the English barons ended up with civil war after Despenser tried to expand his power and influence into Wales, leading to open conflict with the Marcher Lords – those nobles who were tasked with protecting the English–Welsh border. Hugh also interfered in government policy and accumulated lands and wealth through fraud, violence and abuse of power. Contemporary chroniclers – the tabloid press of the day – were scathing. The annals of Newenham Abbey recorded 'the king and his husband fled to Wales', while Jean Froissart didn't beat about the bush when he wrote Despenser 'was a sodomite'. Despenser was eventually seized by the queen and

Roger Mortimer and tried at Hereford for being 'an enemy of the realm and a traitor'. Predictably, he was found guilty and, before being hung, drawn and quartered at the stake, while still conscious he had his penis chopped off and thrown into the fire.

It was during Edward II's ongoing struggles with the English barons that, in 1325, his brother-in-law, Charles IV of France, took advantage of the conflict across the Channel to demand the king paid homage for his Aquitaine territories. Reluctant to leave England, Edward made the 12-year-old Edward of Windsor (whom he had already created Earl of Chester at 12 days old) Duke of Aquitaine and sent him as his representative, escorted by his mother and Mortimer. While in France, Isabella visited Hainault, where she betrothed Prince Edward to Philippa, daughter of William I, Count of Hainault. The queen used money raised in the marriage negotiations, as well as a loan from her brother Charles IV, to raise a mercenary army with the aim of overthrowing Edward II. This would be the first major invasion of England since the Norman Conquest.

When Prince Edward and his mother arrived in England, they were greeted with relief and joy, although, worryingly, in London the thought of overthrowing the present regime led to rioting and looting. The mob even seized the prince's younger brother Prince John from the Tower of London, where he was residing, and set him up as ruler of the city, even though it had never had one, or a right to one. For Prince Edward it must have been an alarming experience since the overwhelming desire to overthrow an anointed king would not only destroy his father's life but would affect the reputation of the Crown and therefore his own future.

Meanwhile, Edward II had fled into Wales, which was taken to mean that he had abandoned his kingdom so, on 26 October 1326, the queen announced that Prince Edward was now to be

'Custos' or guardian of the realm. Two days later writs were issued under his seal as Earl of Chester and Duke of Aquitaine, for parliament to meet in his name. The queen and her lover were clearly using her son's name and position for their own ends. Eleven days earlier, in Wallingford, they issued a proclamation denouncing Edward II for everything from being manipulated by evil men and ruining the reputation of the monarchy to imposing heavy taxes on the people. In Oxford on the same day, Adam Orleton, Bishop of Winchester, condemned the king as 'a tyrant and a sodomite'. As historian Ian Mortimer points out: 'with Mortimer in charge, the outlook for the royal family was bleak.'

On 16 December, King Edward was arrested near Llantrissant in Wales and taken to Kenilworth Castle in Warwickshire. Technically this meant that the anointed King of England was back in his country, invalidating Prince Edward's regency. What was required was the removal of the king, one way or another. Unsurprisingly, Prince Edward did not want his father killed, fearing such a radical solution could be used as a precedent when he reached his majority and was fully in control of the country. The only solution was deposition, which since the king had been anointed in the name of God, had to be treated with sensitivity.

Mortimer started the ball rolling by stirring up public anger in London. Parliament was called in early January 1327 and, after lengthy speeches and sermons, the assembled peers and clergy enthusiastically cried out: 'Away with the king.' On the 15th, Walter Reynolds, Archbishop of Canterbury, once loyal to Edward II, helpfully preached on the text '*vox populi, vox dei*', advocating deposition by the will of the people and of God. Articles of Deposition against the king were proclaimed.

At this point Prince Edward threw a spanner in the works by refusing to meet the assembled barons at Westminster to receive their acclamation. He refused to be proclaimed king if his father had been forced to renounce the throne rather than voluntarily renouncing it. He was not the only one to object. The bishops of Rochester, London and Carlisle all favoured abdication rather than deposition. Crucially, William Melton, Archbishop of York, shared this view. Prince Edward knew Melton well. He had been Controller of the Wardrobe, a key courtier who was in charge of expenditure in the various royal household departments.

Prince Edward was quite possibly influenced by Melton and the others. He made it clear that if his father had to be replaced his preferred method was abdication, perhaps again mindful that deposing an anointed king set a worrying precedent for a future monarch. The prince's firm stance was a sign to parliament and to the ambitious Mortimer that, despite his relative youth, he was not going to be a pushover, either then or in the future.

Mortimer had no alternative but to send a delegation to Kenilworth to tell him of parliament's decision and Prince Edward's reluctance to accept the throne under those circumstances. On 21 January, Edward II appeared in the castle's Great Hall, looking a forlorn figure dressed in black and weeping. He eventually agreed that if he had lost the support of the nobility and the people then the only solution was abdication. The deputation returned to Westminster on the 24th and the following day it was announced that Edward had 'of his own goodwill and by common counsel and assent of the prelates, earls, barons and other nobles and commonality of the kingdom, resigned the government of the realm'. In other words, the reign of Edward III had begun.

Three days later the Great Seal was delivered into the king's hands, and on the 29th the new king informed the sheriffs of his father's abdication and his own succession. He was, he said, taking 'upon us the Government of the said Realm', and more importantly for his own peace of mind and for the sake of the monarchy, he was 'yielding herein to Our Father's good pleasure'. In other words, to him, it was a father–son decision rather than one inflicted on him by the Church, nobles or the overly ambitious Mortimer.

The contemporary *Chronicle of Lanercost* tells us:

Public proclamation was made in the city of London that my lord Edward, son of the late king, was to be crowned at Westminster upon Sunday, being the vigil of the Purification of the Glorious Virgin, [i.e. 1 February] and that he would there assume the diadem of the realm.

It would have been impossible for preparations for the coronation to have been done and dusted in the week between the announcement of Edward II's abdication and the date chosen. There is no definitive timescale of events for decorating the abbey, preparing the royal wardrobe or ordering the usual extravagant amount of food ingredients for the coronation banquet. Historians speculate that Isabella and, more likely, Mortimer, must have had one eye on organising the ceremony since the previous autumn, when Prince Edward was declared Custos.

Certainly, when Edward III entered Westminster Abbey on that Sunday morning, he would have been faced with a dazzling explosion of gold in every direction, from the stage in front of the High Altar covered in quilted gold silk to the throne also decorated in cloth of gold, with golden cushions all positioned beneath a gold canopy. There were also twenty-one tapestries, six other pieces of cloth of gold and twenty-two pieces of cloth of gold on linen. Edward, dressed in red samite (a luxurious heavy silk fabric worn by medieval English monarchs), must have stood out to the assembled nobles and clergy. Prior to his arrival he had walked from Westminster Hall to the north transept door of the abbey barefoot on a striped carpet, supported by ten bishops and walking beneath a purple canopy held aloft by the Cinque Port barons, as the excited crowd jostled within feet to get a better view.

Earlier that morning the young king had been made a knight by Henry of Lancaster who, like Edward II, was a grandson of Henry III. Lancaster was one of the former king's fiercest opponents and had backed Isabella's cause, so it would have been no surprise to Edward III to witness him also knight three of Mortimer's sons on the same day. All the knights were dressed in matching scarlet, red and brown cloth, apart from the Mortimer brothers who were also dressed in cloth of gold, the traditional apparel used by earls. Edward would also have noticed how Mortimer bestowed gifts on his own supporters in the name of the monarch.

One significant change that occurred before Edward's procession set off from Westminster Hall was the revival of the Anglo-Saxon election of the king. In other words, the new monarch was not to be crowned by hereditary right but by the will of the people – or, in reality, by the assembled nobles and clergy. Four earls reported the election of the king to those in the abbey, asking them if the king was to be elected 'ab omni populo' ('by the people'). The archbishop then requested that four bishops and four abbots ask the assembled VIPs if they would validate the report of these four earls. As the answer was in the affirmative, the above clergymen and four knights gave thanks to God and the king was able to be admitted into the precincts.

Little is known about the actual coronation ceremony. We are told by one chronicler that the crown of St Edward 'was of vast size and a great weight' but Edward 'bore it like a man'. While we hear about the Confessor's crown, there is no mention of the St Edward Chair or the Stone of Scone, which was perhaps regarded more as a victory symbol against the Scots than an essential part of the English coronation service. After a request for the Stone's return by its rightful owners in 1328, Edward III ordered it should be sent back to Scotland but this was refused by the then abbot, William de Curtlyngton.

Isabella was seen to weep throughout the service, which the English chronicler Thomas of Walsingham thought was a pretence. Another chronicler, lauding her for removing the corrupt Edward II, refers to her as 'Mother Isabella, our royal noble, prudent, beautiful and excellent star'. Until Edward III reached his majority four years later, the country was very much in her hands, as well as Mortimer's, with the support of parliament and even the pope. One of her first actions was to award herself a pay increase from £4,400 per annum to an unprecedented £13,333, making herself one of the richest land-owners in the country. Adam Murimuth, canon of St Paul's Cathedral, was amazed that 'to her son she left barely the third part of his kingdom'; in other words, he had a third of the royal revenue while Isabella and Mortimer controlled the rest between them.

The day after the coronation a regency council was appointed with Henry of Lancaster as its president and the king's official guardian. It was, of course, a fiction since the real power behind the throne was Isabella, aided by Mortimer. A contemporary illustrated manuscript presented to Edward depicts him and his mother, side by side, both crowned and both enthroned.

In effect, one corrupt regime was replaced by another. 'Roger Mortimer was in such glory and honour that it was without all comparison,' says the *Brut Chronicle*. He 'honoured whom he liked, let the king stand in his presence, was accustomed to walk arrogantly beside him', and even shared the king's plate at dinner, as well as his carriage. Mortimer, continues the chronicle, 'was so proud and high that he held no lord of the realm as his equal' and upset his fellow peers by insisting on being called 'my lord the Earl of March'. Even his own son labelled him 'the King of Folly'.

Edward bided his time until 1330, the year he reached his majority and was able to rule alone, and the same year his wife Philippa of Hainault gave birth to their son, Edward of Woodstock (the future Black Prince). In October that year, Edward, aided by William, Baron Montagu, and a force of twenty-three armed men, invaded Nottingham Castle, where Isabella and Mortimer were in residence. A fight broke out on the stairs and the queen's lover was cornered, leaving Isabella to throw herself at the king's feet crying, 'Fair son, have pity on gentle Mortimer!' Edward did show some pity: after his trial for treason, Mortimer was executed at Tyburn, with Edward magnanimously agreeing not to have him quartered or disembowelled. Edward III was now solely in charge of his realms.

RICHARD II
1377–1400

Richard succeeded his grandfather Edward III at the age of 10. The economic slump following the Black Death combined with the cost of the ongoing war with France led to social unrest, fuelled by the government's legislation keeping wages low despite rising prices. The resulting Peasants' Revolt of 1381, led by Wat Tyler, was ruthlessly put down with some 1,500 rebels killed. Richard ended the conflict with France in 1396. His lack of an heir led to a struggle with the heirs of Edward III, firstly with John of Gaunt and, after his death, with his son Bolingbroke – Henry of Lancaster.

Coronation of Richard II, 16 July 1377

According to the chronicler Thomas Walsingham, Richard II's coronation 'was a day of joy and gladness … the long-awaited day of the renewal of peace'.

It was very 'long awaited' since his grandfather Edward III had reigned for just over fifty years when he died of a stroke at the royal palace of Sheen on 21 June 1377. Richard's father (and the king's eldest son), Edward, the Black Prince, who had helped vanquish the French army at Crécy, had died the previous year from what is thought likely to have been dysentery.

The king's funeral was held at Westminster Abbey on 5 July and the coronation date fixed for eleven days later, on Thursday the 16th. Richard was only 10 at the time of his accession and the urgency of the coronation reflects the peril of a minority. Edward had three surviving royal uncles, the dukes of Lancaster, York and Gloucester, who were all capable military commanders, and ideal leaders for any faction opposing the Crown. The French had already maintained a fleet in the Channel in the last weeks of Edward's life and would land at Winchelsea and Rye on the south coast just a week after the king's death. The series of skirmishes was successfully defeated.

Given that it was half a century since the last such occasion, there was great interest, with people travelling from all over the country to attend or to watch the ceremony. The National Archives holds a list of attendees at the coronation. Adam de Pesales travelled over a hundred miles from Newcastle under Lyme, probably as a retainer to his lord, the Earl of Stafford.

Richard II in his coronation robes seated in the Coronation Chair and holding the orb and sceptre. This wooden panel painting dating from the 1390s is the earliest known portrait of an English monarch.

His visit to the capital was memorable for more than being an eyewitness to history, since on the return home he was mugged by brigands led by Hugh de Wrottesley, who tried to kill him.

Pageantry played a key role in Richard's ceremony. His was the first to feature the eve of coronation procession from the Tower of London to the Palace of Westminster, which became a feature of subsequent coronations for the next 300 years, ending with Charles II in 1661. This must have been a heady experience for the 10-year-old sovereign, who was accompanied by international participants led by men of Bordeaux (where Richard was born at the Archbishop's Palace on the Feast of the Epiphany, 6 January 1367, which probably accounts for contemporary chronicles claiming the presence of three kings – Castile, Navarre and Portugal). Next came representatives of London wards, German mercenaries, men of Gascony and English earls, barons and knights – the latter all dressed in white to complement the king, who was also dressed in white in an outward show of his innocence.

Richard was accompanied by his friend and tutor Simon Burley carrying the Sword of State, while Nicholas Bonde, Knight of the Chamber, guided the king's horse. Near St Paul's Cathedral, John of Gaunt, Duke of Lancaster, had to cut a path for the procession through the packed throngs. A glimpse of royalty was not the only attraction since, for the three-hour duration of the spectacle, conduits flowed with red and white wine. The one at Cheapside was decorated as a castle with four turrets, with a maiden Richard's age clinging to each one. They blew gold leaves on to the boy-king and offered him wine, while an angel descended from the top of the structure proffering a crown of gold. When he did finally make it to the Palace of Westminster, Richard was plied with more wine in Westminster Hall before returning for the night.

The following morning Richard was escorted by his archbishops and other members of the clergy to Westminster Abbey, where his throne awaited him. Richard was no stranger to ceremonial, having already attended the opening of parliament the previous January on behalf of his grandfather.

The young monarch was led to the abbey altar, where he made an offering of a pound of gold and the gift of a new altar frontal. After kneeling in prayer, he swore to uphold the laws and customs of England, as well as promising to protect the Church in an oath that dated from the time of his great-great-grandfather Edward I.

There then followed the ceremony of consecration, during which his white shirt was removed and his chest and shoulders were anointed with holy oil, as well as his hands and head. After this he was presented with the regalia – the ring 'marrying' him to the country, the sword to protect his kingdom and his sceptre. A contemporary portrait of Richard – the earliest known portrait of an English monarch – dating from the 1390s and displayed in the abbey, also shows him holding an orb in his right hand. Unlike later royal orbs, this has a long stem emerging from the top surmounted by a cross.

Usually at this point previous kings would retire to change from their royal robes into less formal dress prior to walking back to Westminster Hall. Richard was an exception. Perhaps because the ceremony was exhausting, coming as it did the day after a lengthy procession through the streets of London, the newly crowned king was carried in all his finery on the shoulders of Simon Burley. A contemporary account tells us they 'went in to the palace by the royal gate with crowds milling all around him and pressing upon him, so that on the way he lost one of the consecrated shoes through his own thoughtlessness'. This was regarded as a bad omen, and perhaps to atone for it, in 1390 Richard sent a pair of red-painted velvet slippers, blessed by Pope Urban VI, to the abbey authorities to be placed with the other pieces of his regalia.

At Westminster Hall, Richard retired to his chamber where he 'spent the rest of that day up until dinnertime in dancing, leaping and solemn minstrelsy for joy at that solemnity'. After dinner, which unsurprisingly left him 'wearied with extreme toil', he retired to bed.

Richard's two wives were both crowned at the abbey. In 1582, aged 15, he married Anne of Bohemia, daughter of the Holy Roman Emperor Charles IV. The ceremony was conducted on 20 January and she was crowned two days later. By then Richard was so short of money he had to pawn the jewels that had once belonged to Eleanor of Aquitaine to pay for a new crown. The king's second marriage, after the untimely death of the queen in 1394, was to Isabella of France in November 1396, when he was 29 and she was five days short of her seventh birthday. Her coronation was held in Westminster Abbey the following January.

HOUSE OF LANCASTER
1399–1461

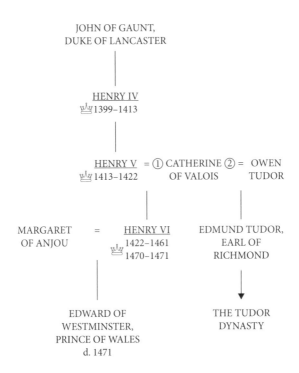

JOHN OF GAUNT,
DUKE OF LANCASTER

HENRY IV
1399–1413

HENRY V = ① CATHERINE ② = OWEN
1413–1422 OF VALOIS TUDOR

MARGARET = HENRY VI EDMUND TUDOR,
OF ANJOU 1422–1461 EARL OF
1470–1471 RICHMOND

EDWARD OF THE TUDOR
WESTMINSTER, DYNASTY
PRINCE OF WALES
d. 1471

HENRY IV
1399–1413

Shakespeare referred to Henry's reign as 'a scrambling and unquiet time'. Having seized the throne, he had to deal, first of all, with a rising from Richard II's half-brother and his nephew, forcing the new king to put Richard's murdered body on display in London to prove he was dead. The Welsh, led by Owain Glyndŵr, rebelled, as did the Scots. Henry also had to contend with a civil war, pitting his troops against the Percy family and Edmund Mortimer, Richard's nominated successor.

Coronation of Henry IV, 13 October 1399

Henry IV was a usurper king with some of his contemporaries, including Charles VI of France, refusing to accept the legitimacy of his rule. In order to boost his claim to the throne, he organised an enthronement ceremony in Westminster Hall two weeks prior to his actual coronation.

Henry Bolingbroke was a first cousin of his predecessor Richard II. Both were grandsons of Edward III of England and were childhood playmates. In 1398 Bolingbroke was banished from the country by the king in order to save his life, since Henry had vowed to fight a duel on behalf of Richard against the Duke of Norfolk who, Bolingbroke had claimed, had made treasonable remarks about the monarch.

The following year Henry's father, John of Gaunt, Duke of Lancaster, died and, for some unexplained reason, the king refused to allow Henry to inherit the Gaunts' lands and assets automatically. Henry returned with a group of supporters aiming to seize his rightful inheritance as Duke of Lancaster, while Richard was away fighting in Ireland. Bolingbroke amassed a sizeable army of 100,000 and decided to seize the throne. Richard was imprisoned in the Tower of London and Henry bypassed the king's nominated heir, Edmund, 5th Earl of March, another descendant of Edward III but with a better claim.

On 29 September 1399, Henry, with a group of nobles and senior clergy, headed for the Tower, where Richard was brought before them. The chronicler Jean Froissart tells us that the king was brought into the hall 'aparelled lyke a king in his robes of estate, his scepter in his hande, and his crowne on his head'.

Richard initially refused to abdicate but, as Henry refused to negotiate, he was compelled to renounce the throne and, according to the *Dieulacres Chronicle*, he took off the crown, 'placed it on the ground and resigned his right to God'. The Archbishop of Canterbury took the crown and placed it in a coffer to take to Westminster Abbey. As if this wasn't enough humiliation, Richard was obliged to read and sign the instrument of abdication, which stated: 'I confess, acknowledge and recognise … that I have been and am entirely inadequate and unequal to the task of ruling and governing the kingdom.' As historian Sir Roy Strong points out, 'this cannot have been anything other than a piece of invented ceremonial'.

The following day, Henry appeared before an assembly of peers and clerics in Westminster Hall. The Archbishop of York read out the account of Richard's abdication and Thomas Arundel, Archbishop of Canterbury, who had accompanied Lancaster's invasion forces, gave a sermon criticising Richard's rule and emphasising the virtues of Henry. According to the chronicler Adam of Usk, Henry had also been given Richard's coronation ring and, more importantly, 'the throne being vacant … the said duke of Lancaster, being raised up to be King, forthwith had enthronement at the hands of the said archbishops'. Henry, seated on the royal throne, which was draped in cloth of gold, read his own statement outlining his right to the throne and pledging to serve. Arundel now dramatically asked the assembled nobles and members of the clergy if they assented to Henry becoming king and they all shouted, 'Yes! Yes! Yes!', while the mood both inside and outside Westminster was described as a 'frenzy'.

Two days before the coronation, Henry processed to the Tower, where in a new departure he invested forty-six of his followers in a new order of chivalry (which would be formally created the Order of the Bath by George I over 300 years later). The ceremony was given its name since the knights, including three of Henry's sons, took a ritual purification bath following an all-night prayer vigil. They were then dressed in long green robes and hats embellished with white cords. The knights joined in the procession from the Tower to Westminster accompanying Henry, who, despite the rain, rode bare-headed on a white charger dressed in a doublet of cloth of gold. He was clearly following parliament's advice that 'nothing which ought to be done should be left undone'.

Henry chose 13 October for his coronation since it was the Feast Day of St Edward the Confessor. Linking himself with the founder of Westminster Abbey was another attempt to elevate himself as the rightful monarch. The date was also relevant since it was exactly a year to the day since he had been exiled to France.

The ceremony had several innovations, including the use of the Sword of Lancaster that Henry had carried with him when he landed at Ravenspurn on the Yorkshire coast. The throne was elevated on a dais and for the first time we hear a mention of the Stone of Scone, which as a symbol of Scottish coronations previously had little significance at the crowning of an English monarch. Henry was very much an English king, speaking this as his first language, so it was the first time since the Conquest that the king made his coronation oath in a language that was not French or Latin.

Another innovation was the use of Thomas Becket's holy oil. Brought to England by the Duke of Brabant for Edward II's coronation, it was never used. It was said to have been given to Becket in a dream by the Virgin Mary during his exile in France in the 1160s. Henry lay stripped to the waist at the High Altar and was anointed on his hands, chest, shoulders, upper back, arms and head. This spiritual blessing from the Almighty did have one unforeseen consequence. According to Adam of Usk, Henry kept a cap on his anointed head for more than a week, which led to him becoming infected with lice and ended up with him losing his hair for a time.

After the coronation Henry walked in procession to Westminster Hall, which by then had the new addition of the hammer-beam roof we see today, made by Richard II's master craftsman Hugh Herland. The royal party, including the king's four sons, two archbishops and seventeen other bishops, as well as the peers of the realm, were served three courses. The first included sturgeon, heron, pheasant and boar's head. The second was led by venison, crane, bittern and pullet, while the third included rabbit, egret, curlew, partridge, peewit, quail, eagle and snipe.

At one point the north door opened and the King's Champion, Sir Thomas Dymoke, rode in on one of Henry's best war horses. In what was by now becoming a tradition, he challenged anyone not believing the crowned guest of honour was the rightful king to fight him in a duel. Presumably there was more tension in the air whenever a usurper was on the throne, though this time Henry broke the awkward silence by announcing: 'If need be, Sir Thomas, I shall personally relieve you of this task.'

HENRY V
1413–1422

Henry V was born on 16 September 1386 at Monmouth Castle and as a boy spent time with his cousin Richard II, who made him a knight. In 1399 he became Prince of Wales at the time of his father's coronation and also Duke of Lancaster in the same year.

In his youth he gained military experience fighting the Welsh prince Owain Glyndŵr and was also present at the Battle of Shrewsbury in 1403, when his father defeated the rebel army of Henry 'Harry Hotspur' Percy.

His short, nine-year reign is best remembered for his military success against the French during the Hundred Years War, including the famous victory in the Battle of Agincourt. By 1420 he had captured large swathes of northern France, including Paris. Under the terms of the Treaty of Troyes, Charles VI of France recognised Henry as regent and heir apparent to the French throne. The same year he married the king's daughter, Catherine of Valois, to cement the alliance. Sadly, Henry never had time to capitalise on his success. He died on 31 August 1422 in France during his final campaign, leaving a widow of 20 and their 9-month-old son, Henry VI.

Henry V is a personal hero of King Charles III. In 1989 The film actor and director Kenneth Branagh sought advice from the then Prince of Wales on what it is to be heir to the throne, prior to directing his film version of Henry V. *Branagh later recalled, 'I met Prince Charles who was very open, particularly about the burdens of expectation, and the fact of isolation, and this to me was very interesting.'*

Coronation of Henry V, 9 April 1413

Very little is known about the coronation service for Henry V, but the contemporary chronicles agree that events surrounding the ceremony amounted to a rite of passage for the 26-year-old king, developing him from a wayward youth into a man of faith and integrity.

For instance, Thomas Walsingham writes that, after the coronation, Henry became 'another man, zealous for honesty, modesty and gravity'. Others date the transformation to the night his father, Henry IV, died. King Henry was planning to go to the Holy Land and visited the abbey to pray before St Edward's Shrine. While he was there, he appears to have had a stroke and was taken to the abbot's house, where he was laid before the fireplace. He recovered consciousness and asked where he was and was told 'Jerusalem', which was, and still is, the name of that chamber. This fulfilled a prophecy that the king would die in Jerusalem. Shakespeare recounts the story of old Henry's death in *Henry IV, Part II*, and also has Prince Henry try on the crown. None of the chroniclers confirm the crown story but, instead, concentrate on another tale. One recounts the prince 'reflected that he was about to inherit his father's kingdom [and] summoned a monk of most exemplary purity to whom he confessed his past sins'. If true, that must have been a weight off his mind since, according to the *Brut Chronicle*, 'before he was king, when he was Prince of Wales, he fell and inclined greatly to riot and drew to wild company'.

Tito Livio Frulovisi, the Italian humanist scholar best known for his biography of Henry in Latin, the *Vita Henrici*

Quinti, said Henry was 'so reformed and amended his life and manners' that 'all his acts were suddenly changed into gravity and discretion'. It also seems to have affected his libido, since Frulovisi admiringly claims that, from the death of Henry IV until his marriage to Catherine of Valois seven years later in June 1420, 'he had no carnal knowledge of any woman'.

This new, virtuous Henry was evident three days later, when he received oaths of allegiance from the nobles who were still in London as parliament had been in session at the time of the late king's death. Henry promised them he would rule for the good of the country, adding melodramatically that if he failed he would prefer to die and be buried.

On Friday 7 April, he made the traditional journey to the Tower of London, where he was received by fifty young men hoping to receive knighthoods. After Mass, the king spent the night in prayer. The following day the nobles were knighted and accompanied him in procession back to Westminster.

Henry must have made an impressive sight in his coronation robes. He was 'very tall [6ft 3in (190.5cm)], slim, with dark hair cropped in a ring above the ears and clean-shaven'. He had a prominent nose and a ruddy complexion, and his eyes 'flashed from the mildness of a dove's to the brilliance of a lion's', depending on his mood.

The ceremony was conducted by Thomas Arundel, Archbishop of Canterbury, who had also crowned the king's father in 1399. Although the details are sketchy, we know the abbey was decorated with cloth of gold and the throne was elevated on a platform in front of the High Altar. Henry is almost certain to have been anointed with the Thomas Becket holy oil used at Henry IV's coronation. When the Virgin Mary offered the oil to Becket in a dream, she very helpfully told him that the kings anointed with it would recover lands lost by their predecessors and that they would regain Normandy and Aquitaine, which must have crossed Henry V's mind when he stormed to victory against the French two years later at Agincourt.

As usual at a Westminster Abbey coronation, not all went to plan. Adam of Usk tells us that the king 'dropped one of his obligatory nobles [not a peer but a gold coin introduced in Edward III's reign] on the floor, and both he himself and those who were present had to search carefully to find it before it could be offered up'.

Even more of a surprise was the unseasonal weather which, Usk recounts, was 'marked by unprecedented storms, with driving snow which covered the country's mountains, burying men and animals and houses and, astonishingly, even inundating the valleys and farmlands, creating great danger and much loss of lives'. London wasn't as badly hit as other parts of the country and the only way it affected the coronation was that the Cinque Port knights had to keep halting the procession from Westminster Hall to shake snow off the silken canopy. While the average fourteenth-century peasant may have worried that the freezing weather was an ill omen, the chroniclers all preferred to think positively that, after this wintry start to the reign, hope and prosperity lay ahead.

It being the fifth Sunday of Lent, the three-course post-coronation banquet was a meat-free affair. Henry's stepmother, Queen Joan of Navarre, sent '2 panniers of Brittany Lampreys' and Sir William Croisier sent a pike. For the loyal Londoners gathered outside Westminster Hall to see the comings and goings, there was the added bonus that the conduit in the Palace Yard ran with red Gascon and Rhine wine.

All seems to have passed off well and an extant letter sent the following Friday from the Bishop of Lewes in London tells the Abbot of Cluny that the new king had succeeded to the throne of Henry IV 'with the unanimous will and consent of all the lords and prelates and with the universal acclaim of the whole nation', or at least from those who weren't under 6ft of snow.

HENRY VI
1422–1461, 1470–1471

Henry VI was the only son of Henry V and Catherine of Valois. He succeeded to the English throne at the age of 9 months, following the death of his father, and became King of France a month later, following the death of his grandfather, Charles VI of France. He was the only monarch to be crowned as king of these dual nations.

During his minority he ruled via a regency council until he came of age at 16 in 1437. An intellectual, timid character who suffered bouts of mental ill-health, he had no aptitude for military leadership, so his reign saw the gradual erosion of English domination in France and the loss of French territories won by his father. In an effort to strengthen the Anglo-French relationship, he married Margaret of Anjou, the niece of Charles VII, but the territorial losses continued and by 1453 only Calais remained under English control.

Opponents led by Richard, Duke of York, criticised the king's mismanagement of the war with France and, after Henry suffered a nervous breakdown in 1453, the political situation spiralled out of control. The thirty-year civil war known as the Wars of the Roses broke out in 1455.

Henry was deposed in March 1461 by Richard of York's son, who proclaimed himself Edward IV. Henry was incarcerated in the Tower of London. He was briefly restored to power in 1470 but Edward resumed control the following year, and on 4 May

1471 Henry's only son, Edward of Westminster, was killed by Yorkist forces at the Battle of Tewkesbury. Just over two weeks later Henry was murdered in the Tower of London on 21 May, probably on Edward IV's instructions.

His lasting legacies are the educational establishments he founded, including Eton College and King's College, Cambridge, and he was co-founder of All Souls College, Oxford.

He made headlines in January 2023 when journalists and historians complained that the Duke of Sussex's autobiography Spare *incorrectly referenced Henry VI as his 'ancestor' and seven times great-grandfather when this is not the case. Prince Harry mentioned the king in a comment about the 'funereal' formal uniform he and generations of Eton scholars are made to wear, since 'we are supposed to be in mourning for old Henry VI'.*

Coronations of Henry VI, 6 November 1429 and 16 December 1431

Henry was born 6 December 1421 at Windsor Castle. His father, Henry V, had already embarked on his final campaign in France, where he died on 31 August 1422, having never seen his son. Seven months later, the baby's maternal grandfather, the French king Charles VI, also died. Under the terms of the 1420 Treaty of Troyes, the two Crowns were to be united and the English king would inherit the French throne. This meant that the 10-month-old Henry was now the first King of France and England, and the youngest monarch to succeed to the English throne.

In September 1423 parliament established a regency council to rule England until Henry came of age. His father's younger brother, John, Duke of Bedford, was made the senior regent with responsibility for the ongoing war with France. During

Above: *Henry VI being crowned at Westminster Abbey in 1429, a month before his eighth birthday and two years before his coronation as King of France in Notre-Dame Cathedral. (British Library)*

Left: *The devout and learned Henry VI from a print after the painting on glass at King's College, Cambridge. Besides founding this academic institution, Henry established Eton College, near Windsor Castle.*

his absences overseas, another paternal uncle, Humphrey, Duke of Gloucester, acted as Lord Protector. Another of Henry V's brothers, Henry Beaufort, Bishop of Winchester, was a member of the regency council.

In April 1429, the teenaged phenomenon Joan of Arc brought a relief army to help defeat the English at the Siege of Orléans, before heading north-eastwards and recapturing French towns and cities from the enemy forces. On 17 July, she brought Charles VII, Henry's rival claimant to the French throne, to Reims, where he was crowned King of France with the 'Maid of Orléans' by his side.

Henry's royal council had already discussed the possibility of crowning their king in France to reassert the English claim to the French throne. First, he would need to be crowned on home territory, and so on 6 November 1429, a month short of his eighth birthday, a coronation ceremony was held at Westminster Abbey.

For the people of London, it was a rare chance to see their boy-king, who was kept in relative isolation, apart from appearing in two processions through the city in 1425 and 1428. The night before the coronation he stayed at the Tower of London, where thirty-two Knights of the Bath were created.

He was carried into the service by his tutor, the Earl of Warwick, but, on the way out, walked in procession flanked by two bishops with Warwick carrying his train.

During the service, having been anointed (again, with the sacred St Thomas Becket oil) and redressed in a velvet robe trimmed with ermine, the king was given the regalia. Two bishops held St Edward's Crown above his head, 'for hyt was ovyr hevy for him, for he was a tender age'.

The traditional coronation rite was adapted to include French influences to show that this was, in effect, part one of a two-part service and the whole would only be complete when

Henry was crowned king in France. Mention was made about Henry's descent from Clovis I and his more recent connection with his grandfather Charles VI.

On St George's Day, 23 April 1430, Henry VI left England to spend almost two years in France. With him were his uncle the Duke of Bedford, his great-uncle Cardinal Beaufort and the bishops of Thérouanne, Norwich, Beauvais and Évreux. He stayed first of all at Calais, until July, before heading for Rouen, where he stayed with his uncle the Duke of Bedford off and on for the next sixteen months. He was staying at Rouen when the trial of Joan of Arc began on 28 March 1431, the day after Palm Sunday, and would no doubt have been aware of her death at the stake on 30 May at the Old Market Place in Rouen.

On Sunday 2 December, four days before his tenth birthday, astride a white horse (regarded as a symbol of sovereignty), Henry VI made his solemn entry into his French capital accompanied by the dukes of Bedford, York, and Warwick. The French chronicler Enguerrand de Monstrelet, who was also present at Joan of Arc's interrogation, has left us a detailed account of Henry's procession through Paris. He had spent two days at the royal abbey of Saint-Denis, north of the city, which, since the tenth century, had been the traditional burial site of French kings. He was preceded by twenty-five trumpeters and an escort of 2,000 to 3,000 people.

As he entered Paris he was greeted by Jacques du Chatelier, Bishop of Paris, followed by Simon Morhier, chief administrative for the Crown, accompanied by representatives of the legal and financial professions. As with the English coronation procession from the Tower to Westminster, the king would have been aware of the specially created tableau showing, among other things, the arms of the city and various allegorical figures. At the Port of Saint-Denis, the ceremonial entrance to the city, Henry saw a huge shield decorated with the arms of the city and a huge silver ship filled with white doves and flowers, which represented the three estates of Parisian society – the clergy, nobility ad peasantry.

Within the city boundary there were more tableaux, some with religious themes based on the life of Christ and the Virgin Mary. One memorable creation showed a depiction of the young king himself, wearing his two crowns and seated beneath a silk canopy emblazoned with the arms of France and England. At this point in the procession Henry also rode beneath a canopy, like the one used in the London procession, which emphasised his royal status.

Traditionally, French kings were crowned in Reims, but as this was again in the hands of French opposition forces, Henry was crowned on 16 December 1431 in Notre-Dame Cathedral. As at Westminster Abbey, the king sat on a raised dais. The stairs leading up to it were covered in blue cloth sewn with a fleur-de-lys pattern, and gold draperies decorated the cathedral walls and pillars.

The service was conducted by his great uncle Henry Beaufort, Cardinal-Bishop of Winchester, who also conducted the Westminster coronation. According to Monstrelet, Beaufort upset the Bishop of Paris by insisting on singing the Mass and conducting a largely English service. The chronicler conceded that at least the singing was of a good standard, perhaps since choristers from the English Chapel Royal had been brought over to join their counterparts from the cathedral.

As with his English coronation, Henry's French ceremony was followed by a lavish banquet, though the cuisine wasn't at its best since, for some reason, the food had all been cooked three days before. Henry stayed in Paris for another week before returning to the French coast via Rouen and Abbeville. He arrived back in England in February 1432, having undertaken his one and only visit to his French kingdom.

It wasn't, however, his last appearance in his coronation robes and regalia. Shortly before his sixteenth birthday, Henry attended a crown-wearing ceremony at Merton Priory on All Saint's Day, 1 November 1437, perhaps to herald his assumption of full royal powers, which was confirmed on 13 November.

Henry married Charles VII's niece, Margaret of Anjou, at Titchfield Abbey on 23 April 1445, one month after her fifteenth birthday. She was warmly received when she arrived in London on 28 May, where, in ceremonies echoing those of a king consort, she stayed at the Tower of London. The following day she processed to Westminster seated in a litter draped in white cloth of gold drawn by two horses, cheered by the people who were fuelled with the red and white wine running from the city conduits. She was dressed in white damask with her hair, as was customary for queen consorts, hanging loosely around her shoulders and kept in place with a coronet decorated with pearls and other precious stones.

HOUSE OF YORK
1461–1485

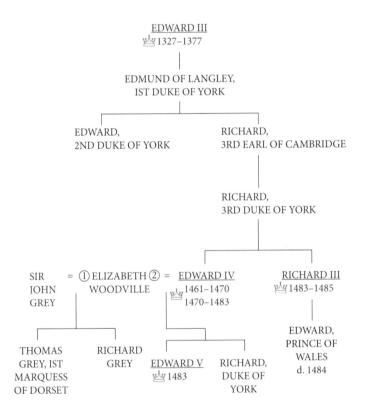

EDWARD III
♛ 1327–1377

EDMUND OF LANGLEY,
1ST DUKE OF YORK

EDWARD,
2ND DUKE OF YORK

RICHARD,
3RD EARL OF CAMBRIDGE

RICHARD,
3RD DUKE OF YORK

SIR
JOHN
GREY
= ① ELIZABETH ② =
WOODVILLE
EDWARD IV
♛ 1461–1470
1470–1483
RICHARD III
♛ 1483–1485

THOMAS
GREY, 1ST
MARQUESS
OF DORSET

RICHARD
GREY

EDWARD V
♛ 1483

RICHARD,
DUKE OF
YORK

EDWARD,
PRINCE OF
WALES
d. 1484

EDWARD IV
1461–1483

A stronger character than Henry VI, Edward IV invaded France to revive England's claim to French territory. Under the terms of the Treaty of Picquigny in 1475, Louis XI agreed to pay 75,000 crowns and an annuity of 50,000 crowns as a bribe to persuade Edward to discontinue his plans to claim the French throne. Edward IV had a large library of books and visited William Caxton to see them produced at England's first ever press in the Almonry area of Westminster, which Caxton set up in 1476.

Coronation of Edward IV, 28 June 1461

The York brothers Edward IV and Richard III downplayed the significance of their actual coronations. The emphasis was instead on their declarations as monarch, which included coronation style rituals involving enthronement, royal robes and public processions. Against the politically fragile world of the Wars of the Roses, the swift ceremony and the more traditional abbey crowning gave both kings a double endorsement by the clergy, the Yorkist nobility and the City of London.

Edward IV's coronation took place while the previously crowned and anointed king, Henry VI, was still alive, having fled to Scotland with his heir Edward, Prince of Wales. His brother Richard's took place when his predecessor, Edward V, was also still alive, imprisoned in the Tower of London.

Edward of York (also known as the Earl of March) was the son of Richard Plantagenet, the Yorkist claimant to the throne during the War of the Roses. Richard was killed at the Battle of

Wakefield on New Year's Eve 1460, leaving 18-year-old Edward as the new head of the Yorkist party.

Early in February 1461, Edward confronted Jasper Tudor, uncle of the future Henry VII, and a Lancastrian force at Mortimer's Cross near Hereford. It was during this battle that Edward encountered a parhelion (also known as a 'sun dog'), an atmospheric phenomenon in which one or two bright spots flank the sun. Edward took this as a good omen and used the three suns as his emblem. It also memorably featured in Shakespeare's *Richard III*, in which the playwright makes a pun on Edward being the son of the late Duke of York:

Now is the winter of our discontent
Made glorious by this sun of York.

Later in the month, the Lancastrian army under Henry VI's redoubtable wife, Margaret of Anjou, was victorious at the Second Battle of St Albans but failed to capitalise on its success by continuing to London, which turned out to be a strategic mistake.

Instead, it was Edward who entered the city at the head of the Yorkist army. He was an imposing figure who could not fail to impress the crowds. At 6ft 4in (193cm), he holds the record as England's tallest monarch. He was fair skinned, good looking and affable, and, according to the Burgundian writer and diplomat Philippe de Commines, 'to the best of my remembrance, my eyes had never beheld a more handsome prince'.

He returned to the family home, Baynard's Castle, situated between Blackfriars and St Paul's Cathedral. On 1 March, the Bishop of Exeter announced the claim of Edward, Earl of March, to be king to a crowd of 4,000 people at St George's Field. When this was approved through popular acclaim, the next day it was proclaimed at various points in the city and, maintaining the momentum, twenty-four hours later the hastily convened King's Council approved Edward's right to replace Henry as king.

The next day, Wednesday 4 March, came his coronation in all but name. In the morning Edward rode to St Paul's Cathedral to make an offering and hear a *Te Deum* before the Bishop of Exeter preached his claim to the throne from the open-air pulpit in the church yard. Then he travelled to Westminster Hall where, before the Archbishop of Canterbury, Thomas Bourchier, he sat on the marble king's bench in royal robes and a cap of maintenance with the sceptre in his hand and was proclaimed king. Edward swore an oath 'that he sholde truly and justly kepe the realme and the laws thereof maynteyne as a true and just kinge'. Afterwards he went in procession to Westminster Abbey, made another offering and heard another *Te Deum*, sat on the throne, and received homage from the peers present. He was not, however, crowned. The message was clearly that public acclamation mattered more than the crowning and anointing by the archbishop.

Between then and the definitive coronation, Edward still had to deal with the ever-present threat from the Lancastrians and headed north to Yorkshire with an army to fight the Battle of Towton, at the end of the month. This was the bloodiest conflict ever fought on English soil, leaving thousands of troops on both sides dead or severely injured. It was a decisive victory for the new king.

It would be another three months before Edward made his triumphant entry into London for the traditional visit to the Tower of London, where he created twenty-eight new Knights of the Bath, including his younger brothers George and Richard.

The following morning, Sunday 28 June, Edward went to Westminster Abbey to be crowned by Bourchier, assisted by William Booth, Archbishop of York. A notably vain character, Edward paid £1,000 to George Darrell, Keeper of the Wardrobe, for 'ready money necessary for our coronation'. After the ceremony, Edward attended the usual banquet in Westminster Hall sitting under a cloth of gold canopy.

The festivities were spread over three days, a welcome distraction from the ongoing civil war for Edward, his supporters, and the people of London. On Monday, the king attended another banquet, held this time at the Bishop of London's Palace in honour of his brother George, whom he had made Duke of Clarence. The celebrations culminated with another public spectacle when Edward, wearing his crown, according to a contemporary chronicler, returned to St Paul's Cathedral 'wishing to pile glory on glory'. The crowds he attracted were as large 'as ever was seen afore in any days'. Edward the showman had scored another victory, albeit a localised one, as the war would rage on for another decade until Henry and the Lancastrian cause were both finally broken.

EDWARD V
10 APRIL 1483–25 JUNE 1483

Edward V was king for only seventy-seven days, the briefest reign since the Norman Conquest apart from Lady Jane Grey, whose nine days as queen regnant is not usually included in the roll of monarchs. His coronation day was proclaimed and postponed twice, so he was never crowned.

As Edward, born on 2 November 1470, was only 12 years old, the executive power during his short reign lay in the hands of the royal council and finally of his uncle Richard, Duke of Gloucester.

Gloucester had the children of Edward IV declared illegitimate and claimed the throne for himself. Edward and his younger brother Richard, Duke of York, were imprisoned in the Tower of London and are known to history as the Princes in the Tower.

Never Crowned

King Edward IV died at the age of 40 on 9 April 1483. His health had deteriorated during the spring but the exact cause of his death is unknown. Realising he was failing, he did have time to add a codicil to his will making his younger brother Richard, Duke of York, regent for his heir.

A royal council met immediately to declare Prince Edward the lawful heir and he succeeded to the throne the day after when this was proclaimed. His mother, Queen Elizabeth, was present at the council but there was then no precedent for a widowed queen consort to act as regent. Nevertheless, the royal council didn't appoint Richard as protector. Instead, they intended to have Edward crowned king as this would avoid the need for a protectorate and the government would be via the council. This happened when Richard II became king at the age of 10 and, later on, a protectorate ruled for Henry VI when he became king at 9 months, lasting until he was crowned at the age of 7.

One of our chief sources for events over this period is the Italian monk Dominic Mancini, who complied a report called *De Occupatione Regni Anglie per Riccardum Tercium* ('The Occupation of the Throne of England by Richard III'), a significant account that only came to light when it was discovered in a library in Lille, France, in 1934. Mancini claims Richard wrote to the council putting forward his claim to be protector under Edward IV's will, but he was too late. By the time it was received the council had set the date of the coronation for 4 May 1483. The queen moved the court to Windsor from 16 to 20 April as preparations for the forthcoming ceremony began.

One consideration was how to pay for the coronation. Edward IV's funeral had cost £1,496 at a time when there had been ongoing and costly conflicts with France and Scotland. The surviving evidence suggests that the boy-king's coronation would be less lavish than his father's had been or his uncle's would be later in the summer of 1483.

Meanwhile, two factions were developing. The queen, born Elizabeth Woodville, was supported by her relatives. Chief among these was the new king's half-brother, the Marquess of Dorset, Elizabeth's son from her first marriage to Sir John Grey. Dorset took control of the Treasury. Meanwhile, Elizabeth's brother, Sir Edward Woodville, was made Admiral of the Fleet with control of the navy. Another brother, Anthony, Earl Rivers, was tasked with bringing the young king back to London in preparation for the coronation, since the Woodvilles were keen to bypass the idea of the protectorate and to control the king via the council. Opposing the Woodville camp was Richard, Duke of Gloucester, and the Duke of Buckingham. Although Buckingham was married to the queen's younger sister, Catherine, he allied himself with Richard's supporters.

In late April, Gloucester and Buckingham arrested Rivers and Lord Richard Grey (another of the young king's half-brothers) as they were preparing to escort Edward to London. They also seized Sir Thomas Vaughan, the king's chamberlain.

Richard now met up with his nephew and showed the deference due to a king, doffing his hat and bowing to the young monarch. Richard was careful not to alarm either the king or the council, promising to rule on Edward's behalf as 'a loyal subject and diligent protector'.

Edward has remained a shadowy figure to history, but Mancini gives us a rare glimpse into his personality when the king declared that he had faith in the council. According to the Italian, Edward claimed:

> he merely had those ministers whom his father had given him, and relying on his father's prudence, he believed that good and faithful ones had been given him. He had seen nothing evil in them and wished to keep them unless otherwise proved evil. As for the government of the kingdom, he had complete confidence in the peers of the realm and the Queen.

Edward would soon realise he should have no confidence in his uncle and Buckingham, and would have no alternative but to acquiesce with their wishes. This became clear when they arrived with Edward in London on 4 May, which should have been his coronation day, but the ceremony was cancelled and the king taken to stay in the Bishop of London's palace.

Queen Elizabeth and Dorset tried to raise an army to recapture her son but lacked a sufficient power base as some of the nobility believed Gloucester had a claim to be protector under the terms of Edward's will and as the boy-king's closest paternal relation. Rather than rushing in all guns blazing, Richard adopted a more subtle approach. He wrote letters to the London corporation declaring his loyalty to his nephew and making it clear he was preventing the Woodvilles from seizing the control of the council for their own advancement.

On 2 May, Edward wrote a reassuring letter to Cardinal Thomas Bourchier, Archbishop of Canterbury, probably under his uncle's instructions, to show that he wasn't being forced from his position.

Queen Elizabeth had by now taken sanctuary at Westminster Abbey with her younger son Richard, Duke of York, and Dorset. All three were based in Abbot Eastney's house in the precincts.

Meanwhile, Richard had an army of 500 to back him up: a significant number to repel a scuffle from any opponents but not large enough to suggest he was attempting a major coup. He was still publicly demonstrating his support for Edward, swearing an oath of allegiance alongside the other nobles and city dignitaries.

On 8 May, the council approved Richard as Lord Protector and for the next seven weeks Edward V and his government was completely in the hands of his uncle. The council, at this point, was still hoping for peace with the queen and for a coronation to end the need for a protectorate. The date chosen was 22 June, when Edward would finally be crowned king and Richard's rule would end. Parliament was summoned to meet three days after the ceremony to approve the arrangement.

At some point in mid-May, Edward was taken to the Tower of London, which, although a fortress, had comfortable suites of rooms for royal guests. It was also, as we have seen, the starting point for a new monarch's procession to Westminster. In order for 9-year-old Richard, Duke of York, to attend the coronation, he would have to join his brother at the Tower, and so Cardinal Bourchier removed him from his mother's custody on 16 June and took him to the king.

Ominously on either that day or the next the coronation was cancelled, and as we shall see, for Richard it was time to pounce.

The fate of the Princes in the Tower has been an endless source of speculation for historians, as well as an inspiration for generations of artists. The two boys were looked after by a physician, possibly John Argentine, who was later physician to Arthur, Prince of Wales, eldest son of Henry VII. Mancini says the doctor reported that Edward, 'like a victim prepared

A touching portrait by Sir John Everett Millais, 1878, depicting the princes in the tower. The boy-king Edward V is on the right wearing the garter of the Order of the Garter beneath his left knee.
(GL Archive/Alamy Stock Photo)

for sacrifice, sought remission of his sins by daily confession and penance, because he believed that death was facing him'. The brothers were seen playing in the grounds of the Tower up to the late summer or early autumn of 1483, when they disappeared from view. The traditional explanation is that they were murdered by their keeper James Tyrell on the instructions of Richard III. This is the version promoted by Thomas More, which Shakespeare adhered to in his 1593 play *Richard III*. This undeniably exculpates the new Tudor regime of Henry VII from any involvement in the deaths, which is put firmly in Richard's hands.

In 1674 the bones of two children were discovered by workmen rebuilding a staircase in the Tower of London. Charles II ordered the remains to be placed in an urn in Westminster Abbey with the names of Edward and Richard on it. Permission for DNA testing of the bones has so far been refused, though there has been speculation that, since Westminster Abbey is a 'royal peculiar' owned by the monarch, Charles III, with his love of history, may one day agree to allow tests on the bones. So, we may be near to determining the fate of the king who was never crowned.

RICHARD III
1483–1485

He was immortalised by Shakespeare for uttering the words, 'A horse! A horse! My kingdom for a horse!' and 'Now is the winter of our discontent'. Some would argue he has also suffered centuries of misrepresentation, not only from the Stratford playwright but from the Tudor apologists, especially Sir Thomas More, who Shakespeare used as source material. From them we are told Richard murdered Henry VI, orchestrated the execution of his brother the Duke of Clarence, may well have poisoned his wife and usurped the throne from his nephew Edward V. Perennially fascinating to conspiracy theorists, Richard made headlines in 2012 when his skeleton was discovered under a car park in Leicester. It was later reburied with due dignity in the nearby cathedral. Elizabeth II wrote that this was 'an event of great national and international significance' and she praised Richard's 'Christian faith [which] sustained him in life and death'.

Richard III and his consort Anne Neville. As a usurper to the throne,
Richard undertook a secular ceremony ahead of the actual crowning
at Westminster Abbey to secure his position as monarch.

Coronation of Richard III, 6 July 1483

Richard III, like his older brother Edward IV, was not a direct heir apparent to the throne and so, again like Edward, he undertook a secular ceremony recognising him as king, ahead of the actual coronation.

Edward IV had died on 9 April 1483 and Richard, Duke of Gloucester, became Lord Protector of the realm, the regent for his 12-year-old nephew, who had succeeded to the throne as Edward V.

On Sunday 22 June, on what should have been Edward's coronation day, Richard was present to hear Dr Ralph Shaa preach a sermon at the open-air pulpit outside St Paul's Cathedral. Shaa claimed Edward IV and Elizabeth were not legally married as the former king was pre-contracted to marry Lady Eleanor Butler. He declared the royal couple's offspring illegitimate, using the biblical text from Solomon about 'bastard slips' from the 'ungodly' not taking root, and Edward V could therefore not be king.

On 25 June, an assembly of lords temporal and spiritual invited Richard to take the throne and he was able to claim that he had been ordained king 'by the concord assent of the Lords and Commons of this Royaume'. Just to be on the safe side, the usurper monarch summoned 6,000 troops from his own estates and those of his main supporter, the Duke of Buckingham, to London in case the people rioted.

There was no insurrection and instead the populace came out in thousands to witness a coronation-style procession from the City to Westminster. Here, like Edward IV before him, he put on royal robes, carried a sceptre and was enthroned on the marble chair of the King's Bench. Beside him stood another ally, John Howard, who was created Duke of Norfolk two days later and also appointed Earl Marshal. It was a secular coronation – a dress rehearsal for the spiritual one that he scheduled for ten days later.

Prior to the abbey service, Richard and his consort, Anne Neville, stayed at the Tower of London, where they hosted a dinner for those to be invested as Knights of the Bath. These men waited on the royal couple and then spent the night in prayer before Richard formally conferred the knighthood on them the following day.

A meat-free dinner was served the next day when the knights waited at the tables. The banquet included 6 dozen lampreys, 112 dozen salt eels, 250 pikes, 16 turbot, 6 halibuts, 600 plaice, 12 conger eels, 12 salmon, 48 soles, as well as crabs, roach and whelks. After this pescatarian feast, Richard and Anne left in a procession in the afternoon from the Tower to Westminster.

A record of the elaborate preparations for the public spectacle, as well as the coronation itself, was compiled. Called the 'Little Device', it formalised the proceedings into a definitive account and would also be the basis for the coronations of Henry VII and Henry VIII. The king, we are told, wore a long gown trimmed with ermine and he sat astride a richly caparisoned horse. He was bareheaded and rode beneath a canopy borne aloft by four knights. He was led by a sword bearer and the newly created Norfolk, as well as by two squires representing the duchies of Guyenne and Normandy. (According to historians Anne Sutton and P.W. Hammond, 'Such [French] representatives appeared in most of the subsequent coronations up to that of George III in 1760, but seem to have first appeared in that of Richard III.')

This was the first joint coronation of a monarch and consort for 175 years, since that of Edward II and Isabella of France in 1308. Queen Anne followed her husband in the procession, sitting in a litter and wearing a kirtle of white damask cloth of gold trimmed with ermine. She wore her hair loose and held in place with a circlet of gold and precious jewels. According to historian Roy Strong, the total cost of their costumes, as well as the abbey decoration and equipage, plus the investiture of their son Edward of Middleham as Prince of Wales in York Minster two months later, came to £3,124 12s ¾d. Prince Edward was a sickly child and was absent from his parents' coronation as, of course, were his cousins Edward V and Richard of York, who were still incarcerated in the Tower of London at the time, before disappearing from public view at some point that summer.

On Sunday 6 July, Richard and Anne walked barefoot on a red carpet from Westminster Hall to the abbey. For his coronation, the king wore a doublet of blue cloth of gold 'wrought with nets and pineapples* and a long gown of purple velvet'. Later he changed into a long gown of purple cloth of gold embroidered with the insignia of the Order of the Garter and the white roses of York.

Anne wore a crimson velvet robe mantle, which was carried by Lady Margaret Beaufort, the mother of Henry Tudor, who would defeat Richard and claim the throne at the Battle of Bosworth two years later. Margaret's husband, Thomas Stanley, attended the king, carrying the great mace in the same procession.

The service followed the traditional running order laid down in the *Liber Regalis* – the recognition, the oath, the anointing, the investing, the crowning and the homage. The officiant was Thomas Bourchier, Archbishop of Canterbury, even though he had promised Edward IV that he would support his heir, Edward of York, as king.

According to Sir Roy Strong, the Little Device contains a misinterpretation of a significant piece of coronation

---

* Not the fruit, which first appeared in Britain in the 1660s, but a reference to pinecones, which were a symbol of resurrection.

regalia worn by the monarch down through the centuries. This is the 'armyll' (armils) referred to now as 'bracelets of sincerity'. A new set, made from 22-carat gold, was created for Elizabeth II's coronation, replacing the pair made for Charles II in 1661. Bracelets were presumably out of fashion for fifteenth-century men since the compilers of the Little Device hazarded a guess that the 'armylls' were 'made up of a stole woven with gold and sett with stones to be putt … abowte the Kinges nek'.

The day ended with a three-course coronation banquet for an estimated 3,000 people in Westminster Hall beginning at 4 p.m., with Richard and Anne seated at a marble table on a dais at the south side of the hall. To feed the multitude, the royal chefs bought in 30 bulls, 100 calves, 140 sheep, 148 peacocks, 218 pigs and 156 deer, all washed down with red and white wine.

During the second course, the King's Champion, Sir Robert Dymock, made his dramatic entrance on horseback to challenge anyone who disputed Richard's right to the throne. Although this is one of the coronations when the champion might have had a taker, no one held their hand up, and Dymock and his steed went home untroubled. There might have been more mouths to feed had not the Duke of Norfolk ridden through the hall on his charger to round up a host of gatecrashers. They probably didn't mind, as outside in Westminster Yard a conduit was spouting free wine for the London crowds.

The banquet must have been a success since the prepared third course was abandoned as the company stayed up later and later during that long summer's evening, before torches were lit and guests departed 'where it liked them best'.

HOUSE OF TUDOR
1485–1603

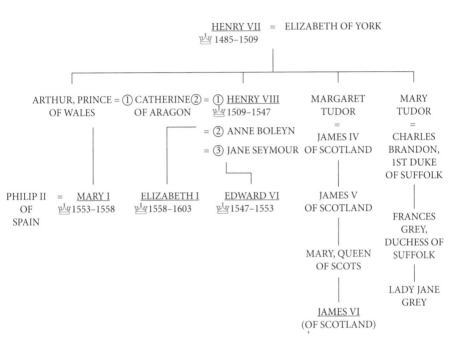

HENRY VII = ELIZABETH OF YORK
♛ 1485–1509

ARTHUR, PRINCE = ① CATHERINE ② = ① HENRY VIII   MARGARET   MARY
OF WALES   OF ARAGON   ♛ 1509–1547   TUDOR   TUDOR
                                  = ② ANNE BOLEYN   =   =
                                  = ③ JANE SEYMOUR   JAMES IV   CHARLES
                                                    OF SCOTLAND   BRANDON,
                                                                  1ST DUKE
                                                                  OF SUFFOLK

PHILIP II = MARY I   ELIZABETH I   EDWARD VI   JAMES V
OF   ♛ 1553–1558   ♛ 1558–1603   ♛ 1547–1553   OF SCOTLAND
SPAIN
                                                                      FRANCES
                                                                      GREY,
                                                          MARY, QUEEN DUCHESS OF
                                                          OF SCOTS   SUFFOLK

                                                          JAMES VI   LADY JANE
                                                          (OF SCOTLAND) GREY

HENRY VII
1485–1509

Henry VII was the founder of the Tudor dynasty and unified the warring factions of the Wars of the Roses by marrying Elizabeth of York. He strengthened his dynasty by marrying his daughter Margaret to James IV of Scotland. Another daughter, Mary, was betrothed to Louis IX of France. His heir Prince Arthur married Catherine of Aragon (who after Arthur's death would go on to marry his younger brother Henry VIII). Skilful at managing his financial affairs, Henry left a full treasury on his death in 1509.

Coronation of Henry VII, 30 October 1485

Henry VII's coronation harked back to the rushed affairs of the early medieval period with the ever-present threat of a rival beating a path to the abbey door.

Henry Tudor had a weak claim to the throne. Having killed the anointed King Richard III at the Battle of Bosworth, he had already sent one potential claimant to the throne – 10-year-old Edward of Warwick – to the Tower of London. His royal descent was pretty tenuous too. His mother, Margaret Beaufort, was a great-granddaughter of Edward III's son, John of Gaunt. On his father's side, the best he could come up with was that his paternal grandmother, Catherine of Valois, was the widow of King Henry V, who had gone on to marry Owen Tudor. As such, having summoned parliament to meet in early November to consolidate his claim to the throne, Henry decided to hold his coronation the week before in an effort to bolster his position.

Considering his later reputation as a skinflint, Henry spared no expense in making his coronation a memorable and glittering occasion. Sir Robert Willoughby de Broke, joint master of the household, ordered cloths, skins, shoes, ribbons and horse trapping, as well as tailors and workmen, at the vast cost of £1,506.

Three days before the ceremony, the king dined with the Archbishop of Canterbury, Thomas Bourchier, who had also crowned both Edward IV and Richard III. In the event, Bourchier was so frail he managed the crowning and anointing but delegated the other parts of the coronation service to his colleagues.

Following tradition, Henry stayed at the Tower of London prior to the service, where, again following precedent, he installed seven new Knights of the Bath.

For his procession to Westminster, he wore a long gown of purple velvet edged with ermine and sat, bareheaded, under a canopy borne aloft by four knights.

In the abbey he was surrounded with loyal supporters including his uncle Jasper Tudor and his stepfather Lord Stanley (recently elevated to Earl of Derby), as well as the Lancastrian bishops of Ely and Exeter. Also present was Henry's mother who, it was noted, 'in all that great triumph and glory wept marvellously'. The only thing that marred the day was the collapse of a stand full of spectators outside the building, but the fact that no one was injured was deemed a good omen.

There followed the usual coronation banquet. The King's Champion, Sir Roger Dymoke, who had provided the same service for Richard III, challenged anyone contesting the new monarch's entitlement to the throne to trial by combat. This must have struck everyone present as ironic given Henry's dodgy claim to the throne, and although no one spoke up on the day, there would be several pretenders to the throne over the next few years, most famously Perkin Warbeck and Lambert Simnel.

Parliament met on 7 November to ratify Henry's claim. According to the *Croyland Chronicle*:

the sovereignty was confirmed to the lord the king as being his due, not by one but by many titles, so that we are to believe he rules most rightfully over the English people, and that not so much by right of blood as of conquest and victory in warfare.

Henry must have breathed a huge sigh of relief when the unequivocal statement was released.

Also strengthening his claim was his marriage to Elizabeth of York, which linked the houses of York and Lancaster and drew a final line under the three-decade Wars of the Roses.

The couple had married on 18 January 1486 and plans for her coronation were drawn up immediately but then postponed, probably due to her pregnancy, which the king would not have wanted to jeopardise. Their son, Prince Arthur, was born only eight months after their wedding, on 20 September. It would be another year before Elizabeth was crowned on the Feast of St Catherine (the patron saint of royal ladies), 25 November 1487.

If anything, Elizabeth's coronation outdid her husband's in splendour. She too stayed at the Tower having journeyed from Greenwich with a whole flotilla of craft, as well as trumpeters and clarions, to Tower Wharf, where she was met by Henry. Fourteen more Knights of the Bath were installed and the following day she processed through the streets of London to Westminster.

She walked in state to the abbey dressed in a purple velvet mantle edged in ermine, her hair down around her face and a bejewelled gold circlet on her head. As was so often the case at coronations, crowd control was an issue. Excited Londoners fought to carve up the carpet she had walked on with disastrous results, as several people were slain in the fracas and Elizabeth's ladies, behind her in the procession, were caught up in it all and were distraught.

Rather sensitively, Henry allowed his wife to hold centre stage and didn't appear publicly. Instead, with his mother alongside, he watched proceedings from behind a screen erected between the High Altar and pulpit. He did the same at the state banquet in Westminster Hall, where the crowned queen sat on a raised table with the archbishop to her right. For the first course she was served with twenty-four dishes to choose from, including frumenty (a wheat porridge), swan, eel and pike, and then a further twenty-seven dishes presented for her second course. Meanwhile, once again, Henry and Margaret Beaufort discreetly watched proceedings from behind a latticed closet window.

HENRY VIII
1509–1547

Henry VIII has been the subject of hundreds of biographies, as well as being played with gusto by a host of actors including Charles Laughton, Richard Burton, Eric Bana, Keith Michell and, of course, Sid James in Carry on Henry.

He is best known for his six marriages, memorably summed up in order of fate, with the rhyme: 'Divorced, beheaded, died. Divorced, beheaded, survived.' He is remembered for his desperate attempts to have his first marriage, to Catherine of Aragon, annulled, which led to his disagreement with the papacy, the Dissolution of the Monasteries and the formation of the Church of England.

He is also recalled for being 'the father of the navy', for playing real tennis, enjoying jousting, speaking French, Spanish and Latin, for playing the lute and harpsichord, for being able to sing from sight and for having a gargantuan appetite.

Coronation of Henry VIII, 24 June 1509

Henry VIII succeeded to the throne at the age of 17, following the death of his father Henry VII on 21 April 1509. He married his first wife, Catherine of Aragon, the widow of his older brother Prince Arthur (who died in 1502) on 11 June, and

The coronation of Henry VIII and Catherine of Aragon in June 1509. In this sixteenth-century woodcut, the couple are dwarfed by their respective badges: the Tudor rose for Henry and the pomegranate of Granada for Catherine.

their coronation as king and queen consort took place in Westminster Abbey two weeks later.

For the people of London, it was an opportunity to see their young, charismatic and undeniably good-looking king in the flesh. At a height of 6ft 2in (1.88m), he was taller than the average man of the period. His waist, according to his first suit of adult armour, was 32in and he had a 39in chest, strong arms and muscular legs.

Thomas More, who at the time of the coronation was MP for Great Yarmouth but would go on to become Henry's chancellor, was one of many who waxed lyrical about the new king: 'Among a thousand noble companions, the king stands out the tallest, and his strength fits his majestic body. There is fiery power in his eyes, beauty in his face, and the colour of roses in his cheeks.'

The Venetian ambassador Sebastian Giustinian was another who seems to have wanted a bromance with the monarch. During his time in England, from 1515 to 1519, he wrote that Henry was 'extremely handsome; nature could not have done more for him. He had a beard which looks like gold and a complexion as delicate and fair as a woman's.' He also recorded that it was the 'prettiest thing in the world to see the King playing tennis, his fair skin glowing through a shirt of the finest texture'.

On 21 June 1509, Henry and Catherine travelled to the Tower of London by royal barge from Greenwich. The following day twenty-six 'honourable persons' arrived to be invested as Knights of the Bath by the king after being purified in ritual baths and keeping an all-night vigil in the Chapel of St John in the White Tower. Among them was Sir Thomas Boleyn, the father of Henry's second wife Anne Boleyn.

The royal couple left the Tower for the traditional procession to Westminster, setting off at four o'clock in the afternoon as it was Midsummer. They journeyed through Cheapside and past Temple Bar to the Strand. Henry wore a doublet of cloth of gold and crimson velvet robes over a gold jacket covered in diamonds, rubies, emeralds and pearls. Around his neck was a baldrick, an ornamental collar studded with more rubies. The crowds, fuelled as usual with free wine flowing through the conduits of the city, loyally cheered from behind railings, while houses along the route were draped in tapestries and hangings.

Behind him in the procession came Queen Catherine. The last time she had processed through the city was prior to her wedding to Prince Arthur. Then she appeared as a Spanish *Infanta*, riding side-saddle on a mule. Now, as queen, she looked demure, carried on a litter and wearing embroidered white satin, and ermine. According to a contemporary account, her hair was 'beautiful and goodly to behold' and held in place by a 'coronet set with many rich orient stones'. Her ladies, wearing blue satin, were on chariots behind her. They included Elizabeth Stafford, sister of the Duke of Buckingham, Margaret Plantagenet, cousin to the king's late mother, and, ominously, Elizabeth Boleyn, the mother of the queen's eventual replacement, Anne Boleyn. Reassuringly for Catherine, she also had her Spanish courtiers, including her confessor, Fray Diego, with whom she had a strong emotional attachment.

Just as the procession passed through Cornhill, the heavens opened and the delicate silk canopy above Catherine's litter offered no protection, so she was obliged to dash from it at Cardinal's Hat Tavern and shelter 'under the hovel of the draper's stalls'. Thomas More made light of this in a coronation poem, but others thought it an ill omen.

Watching the procession pass through Cheapside was Margaret Beaufort, the king's grandmother, who shed tears of pride; she was also present at the coronation ceremony. She had recently lost her only son, Henry VII, and had been the executrix of his will as well as helping to organise her grandson's ceremony. Sadly for him, she passed away five days after the coronation, on 29 June, the day after Henry's eighteenth birthday.

Henry and Catherine arrived at the Palace of Westminster and, after dining, went to pray in the Chapel of St Stephen before sleeping in the Painted Chamber, created by Henry III, which featured the large mural depicting Edward the Confessor's 1042 coronation.

The following morning, the couple left Westminster Hall shortly after eight o'clock, walking to the abbey along a striped cloth strewn with flowers, which the eager crowd tore to shreds for souvenirs the moment the royals had passed by.

Among the guests in the abbey were the king's childhood nurse Anne Luke and his former French teacher Giles Duwes. Thomas More, who was also present, later wrote, 'This day consecrates a young man who is the everlasting glory of our age.' Perhaps it was all the incense, but More seems to have been transported to a higher plane of existence: 'This day is the end of our slavery, the fount of our liberty, the beginning of joy. Now the people, liberated, run before the king with bright faces.'

During the ceremony Henry swore his coronation oath before the Bishop of London. A copy of the oath still exists in the British Library with an amendment handwritten by Henry at some point after the break with Rome. Instead of swearing to preserve the rights and liberties of the 'holie churche', the king changed the wording so that henceforward he, or his successor, would swear to preserve 'the holy churche off ingland' (the holy Church of England). There is no evidence these words were ever used, though they clearly show Henry's mindset after rejecting the Roman Catholic faith.

After his anointing (on his palms, back, chest, both shoulders, elbow and his head) at the High Altar, Henry received the regalia from Archbishop William Warham. The archbishop next anointed Catherine on the head and breast before crowning her with a heavy gold diadem set with sapphires, rubies and pearls. She sat on a throne next to Henry's, although, following protocol that still exists today, hers was slightly lower than the monarch's. As she approached him following her anointing, it was noticed she bowed to him, 'honouring as is right, his majesty'.

Returning to Westminster Hall, Henry and Catherine were seated at the medieval King's High Table. This was made of Purbeck marble on the instruction of Henry III to replace an earlier wooden one, and was used by monarchs for about 300 years. Fragments of it were discovered in 2006 during a renovation project to level six of the stone steps at the south side of the hall.

The newly crowned king and queen were faced with a banquet 'greater than any Caesar had known', with 'sumptuous, fine and delicate meats' in 'plentiful abundance', according to the chronicler Edward Hall.

There then followed several days of jousting at the Palace of Westminster, as Catherine wrote to her father King Ferdinand of Aragon, 'our time is spent in continuous festival'. A pavilion was constructed, covered in tapestries and rich arras cloth, as a royal box to observe the events. Nearby, Hall says, 'there was a curious fountain over which was built a sort of castle with an imperial crown on top and battlements of roses and pomegranates'. The pomegranate appeared on Catherine's heraldic badge, as an ancient symbol for fertility and regeneration. This is clearly poignant in retrospect, since Catherine was unable to give birth to a male heir; her six pregnancies resulted in only one child surviving: the future Mary I.

The day after the jousting finished there was a deer hunt in a specially created 'park' inside the palace tiltyard, with the bloodied carcasses being presented to the queen and her ladies at the end of the day. The celebrations ended when the king was informed of the death of his grandmother.

Fast forward twenty-four years and Henry's second wife, Anne Boleyn, was crowned on Whitsunday, 1 June 1533, when she was six months pregnant with the future Elizabeth I. The historian David Starkey considers Anne's ceremony 'one of the best organised but also one of the best coronations in English history'. It seems to have exceeded the usual pattern of a monarch's enthronement with a four-day celebration.

It began on Thursday 29 June with river pageant to the Tower of London and featured a boat transformed into a huge dragon 'continually moving and casting wildfire'. At 3 p.m., Anne boarded the queen's barge, originally Catherine's but now redecorated with banners, pendants and Anne's heraldic symbol, the white falcon. Trumpeters and other musicians played for the

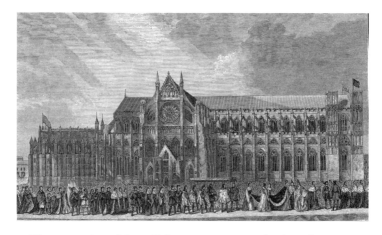

The coronation of Anne Boleyn was a spectacular four-day event, including a river pageant, a procession from the Tower of London to Westminster and, pictured, a majestic progress to the abbey – an ordeal for the queen, who was six months pregnant with the future Elizabeth I. (CBW/Alamy Stock Photo)

queen's delight and, as she approached the Tower where Henry waited to greet her, guns were fired, four at a time, in salute. Having kissed her 'with great reverence and a joyful countenance', Henry escorted her to the royal apartments.

The following day, after the king dubbed eighteen Knights of the Bath, Anne set off at 5 p.m. for her procession through the streets of London dressed, as Catherine had been, in white and wearing a jewelled coronet.

Before her coronation, she walked in a procession to the abbey dressed in a surcoat and with a purple robe carried by the Duchess of Norfolk. Again, Henry was not present.

The ceremony was conducted by Thomas Cranmer, the first Protestant Archbishop of Canterbury. In an unusual move, for the only time in English history a queen consort was crowned with the St Edward's Crown. This appears to have been to legitimise her as the new queen. It was clearly a very messy situation since his marriage to Catherine was only finally annulled on 23 May, some five months after he and Anne conducted a bigamous marriage ceremony and Anne became pregnant.

Anne was escorted back to the palace on the arm of her father Thomas, who had been made Earl of Wiltshire by Henry in 1529. After resting, she emerged for the banquet in her honour. This time Henry did watch, though discreetly from a latticed viewing platform jutting out from St Stephen's cloister. Anne sat in all her regal majesty with two ladies by her side, the Dowager Countess of Oxford and the Countess of Worcester. Their job was 'to hold a fine cloth before the Queen's face when she list to spit or do likewise at her pleasure'. Two more ladies underneath the table had the equally unenviable task of assisting Anne to urinate when required – which was probably often considering her pregnancy.

None of Henry's last four wives had a coronation ceremony. Jane Seymour's was fixed for Sunday 29 October 1536 but in

September the king told the courtier Ralph Sadler that 'the plague had reigned in and in the Abbey itself', adding 'that he stood in suspense whether it were best to put off the time of the coronation for a season'.

Jane did, however, have a river pageant from Greenwich to York Place a few months earlier, on 7 June 1536, complete with trumpets and a forty-one-gun salute from the Tower of London. Henry clearly thought this was the right format for him – perhaps it was a lot less hassle to organise than a coronation – so both Anne of Cleves and Catherine Howard received the Thames pageant treatment. Only his last wife, Catherine Parr, lost out altogether. She had to make do with just having a proclamation in front of courtiers at Hampton Court on the day of her wedding, so no river pageant, no cheering crowds and definitely no consort's crown, sceptre or ivory rod.

EDWARD VI
1547–1553

Henry VIII's much longed-for heir, Edward VI, succeeded to the throne at the age of 9. Due to his tender age, the country was governed by his uncle, Edward Seymour, who became Lord Protector of the Realm and he made himself Duke of Somerset. Seymour became increasingly unpopular with the king's council and was ousted in 1549, being replaced by John Dudley, 1st Duke of Northumberland. Edward's short reign is noted for turning England into an increasingly Protestant country. Thomas Cranmer's 1549 Book of Common Prayer brought uniformity of worship to the state.

Coronation of Edward VI, 20 February 1547

Edward VI was the first monarch to be anointed as Supreme Head of the English Church in a service that was fervently anti-Catholic. As a concession to the king's youth, the service was shortened from the usual eleven to twelve hours to a more manageable nine, though combined with a four-hour banquet, it was still an ordeal for a 9-year-old boy.

Henry VIII died shortly before midnight on 28 January 1547 at the age of 55. 'Loth to hear any mention of death', in the face of the inevitable he left this world holding the hand of his friend Thomas Cranmer, Archbishop of Canterbury.

At 3 a.m. Edward Seymour, 1st Duke of Somerset and brother of Henry's third wife Jane Seymour, rode to Hertford, where his nephew, and heir to the throne, Edward was living. The prince was taken to Enfield to join his sister Princess Elizabeth and it was here that the news was broken to him that his father was dead and that he was now king.

Henry's death was kept secret until Monday 31 January, when it was announced in parliament, and then to the public. The news was already out when Edward and Seymour arrived in London, where the 'nobility of his realm were ready to receive him, to their great joy and comfort'. The new king was also received with a gun salute at the Tower of London, which had been prepared 'with richly hung and garnished apartments' for his use.

On 16 February, Henry was buried in a small vault at St George's Chapel, Windsor, next to his third wife, Edward's mother Jane Seymour. The couple were joined 102 years later by a third occupant, Charles I.

In London, preparations were made for the first coronation in almost forty years. On 12 February, the King's Council had sanctioned a payment of £442 10s for the coronation, a modest amount compared to the £1,039 9s 7d granted to pay for the late king's funeral.

One early decision was to truncate 'the tedious length' of the coronation, 'which should weary and be hurtsome peradventure to the King's majesty, being yet of tender age'.

Before the ceremony, the young king had to endure the traditional four-hour procession from the Tower of London to Westminster. Edward appeared on horseback in the courtyard of the Tower just before one o'clock on Saturday 19 February. He was elaborately attired in a silver gown embellished with 'a girdle of white velvet wrought in Venice silver' garnished with rubies and diamonds and a matching white cap similarly studded with 'like stones and pearls'. His horse was caparisoned in crimson satin sewn with gold damask and pearls. Initially horse and rider sat beneath a canopy held by six mounted noblemen, which hid the child monarch until it was decided he should ride in front of his escort.

The Lord Protector rode ahead of the king, near to the Marquess of Dorset, carrying the Sword of State. Behind the royal party were several thousand men of arms, yeomen of the guard and grooms of the Privy Chamber.

Thousands of Londoners crowded behind the rails on either side of the freshly gravelled streets, kept in check by gentlemen pensioners and law clerks on foot as well as on horseback. Above them the window frames and balconies were draped with rich wall hangings and cloth of gold. The conduits in Cheapside, St Paul's and Fleet Street once again flowed with claret and white wine, which may have helped boost the renditions of a song that was repeated all day and eventually well into the night:

Sing up, heart, sing up, heart, and sing no more down,
For joy of King Edward that weareth the Crown.

The royal procession continually halted to view tableaux with worthy subjects – little boys dressed as Grace, Nature, Fortune and Charity, girls correspondingly dressed as England, Regality, Justice, Mercy and Truth, and women representing the seven liberal sciences. By the time Edward reached a display representing Edward the Confessor, St George on horseback and 'a fair maiden holding a lamb on a string', the procession failed to stop. More to the boy-king's liking was a Spanish acrobat who abseiled down a rope 'as great as the cable of a ship' attached at one end to the spire of old St Paul's Cathedral and anchored at the other end to the gate of the dean's house. The man from Aragon kissed the king's foot before hauling himself skyward for more gymnastics above the churchyard. This was more to Edward's taste and he stayed 'a good space of time'.

He also halted when the mayor and aldermen presented him with purse containing 1,000 crowns. Then as now, royalty didn't carry money and Edward asked his uncle 'why do they give me this' and was told by Seymour, 'It is the custom.' Receiving it was one thing, carrying it while trying to hold the reins and doff his cap to the crowd was quite another, and more than the 9-year-old could cope with, so he passed his cash to the Captain of the Guard, which, according to the official chronicler, caused great offence with the civic worthies.

The next morning peers began arriving at the abbey from 7 a.m., while Edward arrived between 9 and 10 a.m. Like his predecessors, he walked from Westminster Hall accompanied by four dukes – Somerset carrying the crown, Suffolk the orb, Dorset the sceptre and Warwick the king's train.

Having been met at the West Door by the dean, Edward processed to St Edward's Chair before Archbishop Cranmer proclaimed him king. The 9-year-old then walked to the High Altar, where he prostrated himself on the floor at the bottom of the steps while the litany was said. He then changed into a coat of crimson satin with a cap of gold. While he was in the side chapel getting ready, a general pardon was issued for prisoners (apart from the Catholic Duke of Norfolk, who was the main rival to Edward Seymour for the position of regent, and who had been imprisoned for treason shortly before Henry's death).

Edward was given unction on the arms, breast, back, forehead and hands then, thoroughly anointed, he received the royal regalia. Unusually, he was crowned three times: firstly, with St Edward's Crown – an antique gold circlet; then with the Imperial State Crown, which was considered too sacred to be altered for the young king and so was suspended over his head instead; and, finally, with a specially produced, smaller, personal crown.

The Roman Catholic elements of the service were omitted and Cranmer proclaimed Edward 'Supreme Head of the Church elected by God and only commanded by Him'. The archbishop's sermon compared Edward to the Old Testament King Josiah, who wiped out idolatry, and, the primate hammered home his message: 'England must stand inviolate against any intrusion from papal authority.' Indeed, during his short six-year reign, this theme was taken up across the land, with churches having their ornately decorated walls whitewashed and the Latin Mass being replaced by the Prayer Book in the Vernacular. With the devout Edward at the helm, England moved vigorously towards becoming a totally Protestant nation.

His faith was even on Edward's mind as he left the abbey to walk in procession back to Westminster Hall. As he walked, he asked why there were three swords borne aloft before him. Having been told they represented his three kingdoms, he declared, 'One is wanting – the Bible, the sword of the spirit', and commanded it should be brought from the lectern and carried with his earthly ones.

There was still no rest for the newly crowned sovereign, who then had to endure a four-hour banquet still wearing his robe and crown, before having to greet his ministers of state, the foreign envoys and the Knights of the Garter, as well as watching the Masque of Orpheus. As if that wasn't enough, the following days saw jousting tournaments and a series of sermons by clergymen, eager to ingratiate themselves with the new regime. Their themes were unrelentingly pro-Protestant and, as the Roman Catholic Spanish ambassador noted ruefully, the clerics were desperate 'to vie with one another in abusing the old religion'.

MARY I
1553–1558

Mary Tudor was also known as Bloody Mary for condemning over 280 Protestant dissenters to be burned at the stake during her five-year reign. She was the only surviving child of Henry VIII's marriage to Catherine of Aragon and was England's first queen regnant. Her re-establishment of Roman Catholicism was reversed by her half-sister Elizabeth I, who succeeded her in 1558.

Coronation of Mary I, 1 October 1553

Henry VIII's much longed-for male heir, Edward VI, died from a lung infection at the age of 15 on 6 July 1553, though not before overruling his father's 1544 Act of Succession. The act stipulated that in the event of Edward's death without issue, the throne would pass to his half-sister Mary and, should she also die without issue, to Henry's younger daughter Elizabeth.

The dying boy-king, influenced by the Duke of Northumberland, who was the head of the king's council, disinherited his two sisters and declared his distant cousin Lady Jane Grey as his successor. Jane was a great-granddaughter of Henry VII via his daughter Mary, Duchess of Suffolk. More importantly to the fervently Protestant Edward, she shared his faith.

While Mary declared herself queen 'by divine and human law' to her household on 9 July, the following day Jane was proclaimed queen by Northumberland. By 12 July, Mary had the backing of a number of Catholic supporters and assembled a force of around sixty loyalists at Framlingham Castle in Suffolk. Meanwhile, support for Jane collapsed and she was deposed on 19 July, the same day Mary was declared queen in London.

On 3 August, Mary made a triumphal entry into the capital accompanied by an escort of over 800 members of the nobility and gentry.

A month later Mary made it clear to the imperial ambassador that she aimed to restore relations with the papacy 'as they were before the changes we know of took place'. She also released the Roman Catholic Duke of Norfolk and Stephen Gardiner, Bishop of Winchester, before imprisoning the Protestant archbishops of Canterbury and York.

Preparations for the coronation of the country's first queen regnant began in earnest. The 'Liber Regalis' and Little Device, which had been the blueprint for coronations since Richard III's accession, only gave advice on the procession and crowning of queen consorts. The rules had to be adapted and Mary wanted the service to be adapted by Gardiner to reflect her fervently anti-Protestant faith.

On 27 September, Mary embarked at the head of a flotilla of craft along the Thames from Whitehall to the Tower of London accompanied by Princess Elizabeth and their only surviving stepmother, Anne of Cleves.

At the Tower, they were greeted by musicians, singers, trumpets and gun salutes. Inside, the queen rehearsed for her coronation, familiarising herself with the oaths as well as the robes and regalia.

At 3 p.m. on 29 September, Mary left the Tower for the now traditional procession through 1½ miles (2.4km) of narrow streets to Westminster. The queen, seated on a litter drawn by six horses, was 'richly apparelled with mantle and kirtle of cloth of gold ... according to precedents'. On her head was a jewelled crown 'so massy and ponderous that she was fain to bear up her head with her hands'.

As usual, the city's conduits flowed with wine, the crowd was held back behind wooden railings and the houses on the route were draped with banners. There were pageants, orations, musical entertainment and a brief stop at St Paul's to receive £1,000 in gold coins from the Lord Mayor. Unlike Elizabeth I, who, as we shall see, responded graciously to the crowds and festivities, Mary was less effusive. On her official welcome into the city in August, she had listened to an oration given by a hundred poor children and, according to an eyewitness, 'she sayd nothinge to them'. If she 'sayd' anything positive at her coronation parade, it was not documented.

One reason for her downbeat attitude was the threat of anti-Catholic riots. Simon Renard, the imperial ambassador, noted days earlier that there were rumours 'arquebusers, arrows and other weapins were being collected in various houses' and there were fears 'some attempt might be made against [Mary's] person'. In the event, the procession went without a hitch.

At 11 a.m. on 1 October, Mary arrived at the south transept door of Westminster Abbey wearing the crimson robes of a male monarch. Inside, a raised walkway led to a dais, on top of which was a flight of stapes leading to the Coronation Chair.

At each of the four corners of the dais, Gardiner presented the queen as 'rightful and undoubted inheritrix' to the congregation, to which they shouted their affirmation, 'Yea, yea, yea! God Save Queen Mary!' After prayers, a sermon and the oath, Mary changed into a plain petticoat of purple velvet for the anointing on her shoulders, breast, forehead and temple. Only the bishop and the monarch knew that Mary considered the holy oil prepared for Edward's coronation as sullied and had secretly acquired chrism consecrated by the Catholic Bishop of Arras.

At this point, the queen changed into robes of state and received at the altar the regalia, including the crown of Edward the Confessor, the Imperial Crown and one specially made for her, with two simple arches, a large fleur-de-lys and crosses. In another nod to her position as queen regnant, the spurs normally presented to the king to be worn were merely touched by the queen. Also, Mary was handed the sceptre of a queen consort, which, unlike the king's, was surmounted with a dove.

The newly crowned and anointed queen left the abbey at 4 p.m. – 'she twirled and turned [the sceptre] in her hand' – and walked in procession to Westminster Hall. Here she sat with Gardiner to her immediate left and Elizabeth and Anne of Cleves some distance to her right, while 'she rested her feet on two of her ladies'. If she didn't need to rest before the banquet, she would have needed to afterwards, since she was presented with 312 dishes for her own consumption, while a total of 7,112 others were handed round to the other guests, of which 4,900 were wasted.

ELIZABETH I
1558–1603

Elizabeth I, the last of the Tudors, inherited her father's intellect, reading the classics and history books as well as speaking at least six languages. She liked to write poetry and could play the lute and the virginals. She also enjoyed horse riding and hunting. A more moderate Protestant than her brother, she undid the Church legislation imposed by Mary I. In foreign policy Elizabeth sent an army to help the French Protestants after the massacre of the Huguenots and her navy successfully defeated the Spanish Armada. Hers was an era of great adventurers – John Hawkins, Francis Drake, Walter Raleigh – as well as of cultural icons including Shakespeare, Christopher Marlowe, Philip Sidney, Edmund Spencer and Francis Bacon.

Coronation of Elizabeth I, 15 January 1559

The ever-practical Elizabeth II sought the aid of meteorologists to select the perfect day for her coronation. They chose 2 June, which statistically was most likely to have clement weather. Like generations of forecasters, before and after, they got it spectacularly wrong and it memorably bucketed down.

Elizabeth I looked far beyond the clouds to choose her coronation date, instructing John Dee, her astrological and scientific advisor, to study the motions of the earth, moon, planets and satellites to come up with a propitious alignment. He reported back that 15 January augured well.

Bloody Mary died childless on 17 November 1558 and her younger sister Elizabeth succeeded her as monarch at the age

This painting, known as 'The Coronation portrait', shows Elizabeth I crowned, adorned in the cloth of gold that she wore at her coronation on 15 January 1559, previously worn by Mary. (Ian Dagnall Computing/Alamy Stock Photo)

of 25, curiously the same age Elizabeth II was at the time of her accession. The new queen remained at Hatfield House, where she had spent most of her childhood, for the next six days. Wasting no time, on her accession day, she discussed the appointment of commissioners for her coronation.

The commissioners helped create a three-day spectacle, which began on 13 January with a river pageant along the Thames from Whitehall Palace to the Tower of London, where traditionally monarchs spent the night before their progress to Westminster Hall. The flotilla was led by Elizabeth in her state barge and was so impressive it reminded an Italian envoy of the Fèsta de ła Sènsa, the procession of elaborately decorated craft on the Grand Canal of Venice marking the Feast of the Ascension.

On Saturday, the queen's court gathered at the Tower to see her leave in procession for Westminster. More than a thousand people took part, beginning with the lowliest messenger of the queen's privy chamber and her personal servants through to the great officers of state: the Lord Privy Seal, the Lord Keeper of the Great Seal and so on.

Finally came Elizabeth, dressed in a robe of cloth of gold and wearing the crown of a princess, seated beneath a canopy borne by two knights on either side. Her litter was drawn by two mules also covered in gold brocade. The queen would spend some £4,000 on cloth of gold, velvets and satins for the coronation and the whole event, excluding the banquet, cost her £16,741.

The visiting Italian envoy wrote beforehand: 'They are preparing here for the coronation, and work both day and night, on holidays and weekdays.' It wasn't just Westminster Hall and the abbey that were being prepared. The processional route east of St Paul's Cathedral, from Fenchurch Street to Cheapside, was decorated with wooden rails draped in cloths and hung with tapestries.

Five pageants were performed for Elizabeth's entertainment on this eve of coronation celebration. The first showed her genealogy, emphasising her Englishness in contrast to the half-Spanish Mary I, with depictions of her grandparents Henry VII and Elizabeth of York, her parents Henry VIII and Anne Boleyn (thankfully re-headed) and finally topped with Elizabeth standing triumphant and alone. The second pageant depicted the virtues of good governance: 'Pure Religion, Love of Subjects, Wisdom and Justice, which did tread their contrary vices under their feet.'

The third pageant was at the upper end of Cheapside, where the queen received a purse of crimson satin with a thousand marks in gold, emphasising the link between the City and the Crown. Elizabeth responded: 'I thank my Lord Mayor, his brethren and you all. And whereas your request is that I should continue your good Lady and Queen, be ye ensured that I will be as good unto you as ever queen was unto her people.' Her impromptu words were enthusiastically received by the crowd: 'the heartiness thereof was so wonderful.'

The fourth pageant focused on the queen's Protestant faith, with the figure of Truth presenting her with a Bible written in English. Elizabeth took the Bible, kissed it, held it up in both her hands and laid it on her breast.

The final pageant anticipated the future. It depicted her as the Old Testament prophet Deborah, the only female judge in the Bible, who gave peace to Israel for forty years. It was a prescient note to end on, since Elizabeth's reign of almost forty-five years was the longest of the Tudor dynasty.

Elizabeth's pre-coronation procession showed her undoubted skill at public relations. The ease and spontaneity with which Elizabeth related to the crowds was remarked on by eyewitnesses and contemporary accounts. She frequently halted her litter to accept nosegays, and at Fleet Street was handed a branch of rosemary by an old woman, which was still in place alongside her when she arrived at Westminster. Just as Charles III has become adept at glad-handing the crowds on his walkabouts as monarch, so Elizabeth I bridged the gap between monarch and people, not with handshakes but with arms outstretched to salute the people at the back and words of greeting to those nearest. 'Her Grace,' one observer recorded, 'by holding up her hands and merry countenance to such as stood far off, and most tender and gentle language to those that stood nigh … did declare herself thankfully to receive her people's goodwill.'

In another touch reminiscent of the present royal family, Elizabeth bonded with the younger generation. At Temple Bar, the ceremonial entrance to the City of London from the City of Westminster, the queen paused to hear a children's choir and afterwards promised them: 'Be ye well assured I will stand your good Queen.'

The following morning Elizabeth processed on foot, from Westminster Hall, the short distance to the abbey. She was flanked by the earls of Pembroke and Shrewsbury and followed by the Duchess of Norfolk carrying the queen's train. At this point, euphoria got the better of the crowd and, as the young monarch passed by, people dived on the blue carpet her feet had just graced and tore it into shreds for souvenirs. Pandemonium broke out and the Duchess of Norfolk nearly fell over the frenzied scavengers. There is no record of Elizabeth being perturbed.

One thing that did perturb her, though, was the lack of a Protestant Archbishop of Canterbury. The previous incumbent, Reginald Pole (who was also the last Roman Catholic primate), died just twelve hours after Queen Mary, and it took almost a year for the position to be filled by an Anglican. Other possible candidates, including the Archbishop of York and the bishops of London, Winchester and Durham, chose not to take part, and so it was Bishop Owen Oglethorpe of Carlisle, a former chaplain to Elizabeth's stepmother, Anne of Cleves, who performed the service. The coronation took place at a time of bitter division between Catholics and Protestants before the Elizabethan Religious Settlement ended this religious turmoil by redefining the Church of England with Elizabeth as its Supreme Governor.

Hers was the last coronation to be conducted according to the Latin service of medieval times, and Elizabeth is said to have withdrawn to St Edward's Chapel, possibly to avoid participating in Holy Communion. In 1571 she reportedly told the French ambassador that 'she had been crowned and anointed according to the ceremonies of the Catholic church and by Catholic bishops without, however, attending mass'.

Elizabeth did ensure her coronation oath was unequivocally Protestant. She promised to rule according to 'true profession of the Gospel established in this kingdom'. She was also crowned three times by Oglethorpe, first with the Crown of St Edward, then the State Crown and finally a smaller crown, which may well have been the one made for her mother Anne Boleyn's coronation.

Elizabeth's is the first time we have a visual plan of a monarch's coronation. Pen and ink drawings survive showing the raised theatre area of the abbey where the actual crowning took place, at the crossing where the Quire and the north and south transepts meet. Twenty steps led up to an octagonal dais on another five steps, surmounted by St Edward's Chair, high above the congregation.

After the crowning, Elizabeth changed from her coronation gown into a 'rich mantle and surcoat of purple velvet furred with ermines', in preparation for leaving the abbey. The London populace was still out in force and the queen once more played to the crowds, beaming and greeting them. One eyewitness, the Mantuan envoy Il Schifanoya, sniffed that 'she returned very cheerfully, with a most smiling countenance for every one, giving them a thousand greetings, so that in my opinion … [this] exceeded the bounds of gravity and decorum'.

Back at Westminster Hall there was more formality as Elizabeth again sat on high, enthroned on a dais approached by steps and beneath a cloth of estate. Four large tables accommodated the 200 guests and at one end a tiered display table featured 140 gold and silver cups. It was organised by the Duke of Norfolk and his heir the Earl of Arundel, who supervised events in the capacious hall while on horseback. Following tradition, Sir Edward Dymoke, the Queen's Champion, also rode into Westminster Hall and threw down his gauntlet to challenge anyone who did not recognise Elizabeth as monarch and, following the same tradition, no one did.

The festivities included a masque and lasted for six hours until 9 p.m., when Elizabeth retired to Whitehall Palace for the night. The following morning's joust in her honour was postponed as she was 'feeling rather tired'.

HOUSE OF STUART
1603–1714

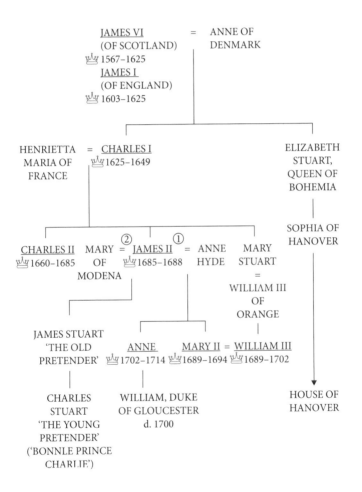

JAMES VI
(OF SCOTLAND)
♛ 1567–1625
JAMES I
(OF ENGLAND)
♛ 1603–1625

= ANNE OF
DENMARK

HENRIETTA
MARIA OF
FRANCE

= CHARLES I
♛ 1625–1649

ELIZABETH
STUART,
QUEEN OF
BOHEMIA

SOPHIA OF
HANOVER

CHARLES II
♛ 1660–1685

MARY
OF
MODENA

② = JAMES II
♛ 1685–1688

= ANNE
HYDE

MARY
STUART
=
WILLIAM III
OF
ORANGE

JAMES STUART
'THE OLD
PRETENDER'

ANNE
♛ 1702–1714

MARY II =
♛ 1689–1694

WILLIAM III
♛ 1689–1702

HOUSE OF
HANOVER

CHARLES
STUART
'THE YOUNG
PRETENDER'
('BONNLE PRINCE
CHARLIE')

WILLIAM, DUKE
OF GLOUCESTER
d. 1700

JAMES VI & I
1567–1625

The clue is in his titles: James was two kings in one. Born on 19 June 1566, the only child of Mary, Queen of Scots, James was crowned king the following summer. His reign of fifty-seven years and 246 days makes him the fourth-longest-reigning British monarch. He is remembered for uniting the kingdoms of Scotland, England and Ireland following the death of Elizabeth I in 1603, for sponsoring the authorised King James version of the Bible and for very nearly getting blown to smithereens thanks to the Gunpowder Plot of 1605.

Coronations of James VI & I, 29 July 1567 and 25 July 1603

James was anointed King of Scotland on 29 July 1567 at the age of 13 months following the abdication of his mother, Mary, Queen of Scots just five days earlier. Mary, whose popularity was already on the wane, had incurred the wrath of her subjects by marrying the Earl of Bothwell, widely suspected of killing her second husband, Lord Darnley. Mother and son were briefly reunited at Stirling Castle (where she herself had been crowned at the age of just 9 months in 1543) in April of the same year, and they would never meet again.

The ceremony was held at the Church of the Holy Rude in Stirling and the infant king was carried from the castle in the arms of Annabell Murray, Countess of Mar. The child was swaddled in coronation robes of crimson and blue velvet made by James Inglis, who had been appointed tailor to the future monarch by Mary the previous January.

Despite being baptised a Roman Catholic seven months earlier, James was given a Protestant coronation. The sermon was preached by John Knox, the religious reformer, who had denounced Mary and backed the rebellion that had led to her eventual removal. He chose as his theme the apt story of the biblical child-king Joash, who was crowned king of Judah and whose mother Athaliah was slain with a sword.

Fast forward thirty-six years and at some point between two and three o'clock on the morning of 24 March 1603, Elizabeth I of England breathed her last at Richmond Palace at the age of 69. By ten o'clock her principal private secretary, Sir Robert Cecil, had proclaimed the queen's first cousin twice removed, James VI, as King of England. An hour earlier the soldier and courtier Sir Robert Carey left Richmond and rode like a maniac to Scotland, arriving at Edinburgh in just two days, despite being thrown from his horse at one point. He took with him a sapphire ring that had been sent to his sister, Lady Scrope, by King James with instructions to return it to him as a sign that Elizabeth had died, and that he was therefore now the King of England.

James had never set foot on English soil in all his thirty-six years, and once he had crossed the border in April 1603 he would never again see the land of his birth.

His last public appearance in Scotland was at divine worship in St Giles's Cathedral, Edinburgh, on the morning of Sunday 3 April. His journey to London was to be a deliberately leisurely one since, as a mark of respect, he purposely wanted to wait until after Elizabeth's funeral on the 29th. He was offered hospitality at a variety of venues from the Deanery at Durham to the Duke of Rutland's Belvoir Castle. At Hinchinbrook he stayed at the home of Oliver Cromwell, uncle of the Lord Protector, and also in the less majestic Bear Inn at Doncaster.

As the king neared London, curious onlookers, eager to see their new monarch, lined the route and James would occasionally have to pause his procession in case people were trampled on. The lawyer Roger Wilbraham, who as Master of Requests controlled the presentation of petitions, requests and appeals to the king or his royal council, estimated 40,000 citizens were trying to attend James's court. He recorded a flood of requests for favours, writing that he was 'swarmed' by petitioners 'at every back gate and privy door' along the route. An extra hundred thousand people were said to have journeyed to the City of London to see James's arrival.

The king journeyed to the Tower of London to await the arrival of his consort, Queen Anne of Denmark, and their two older children, Prince Henry, aged 9, and 7-year-old Princess Elizabeth. Their younger son, the 2½-year-old future Charles I, was considered too sickly to leave Scotland. It was a wise precaution to leave the infant behind since an outbreak of bubonic plague had started to sweep through London. James and Anne, like Elizabeth II and the Duke of Edinburgh 400 years later, left the capital for the relative safety of the crowd-free Windsor Castle.

During his journey southwards, James had agreed on the choice of 25 July, the day of St James the Apostle, for his coronation. As the day neared there were fears it may have to be postponed as the 1603 plague killed 30,000 people – one-fifth of London's inhabitants. But in the end, it was decided to go ahead with an abridged service and the postponement of the traditional procession to Westminster from the Tower.

On Sunday 24 July, the king and queen moved to the Palace of Whitehall for the installation of new Knights of the Bath. The following morning, they took a gilded barge the short distance on the Thames from the steps of Whitehall to Westminster before walking from Westminster Hall to the abbey. Despite heavy rain and the fear of contagion, there were still many onlookers keen to see the first coronation in over forty years. There was no chance of any of them mobbing the king, as they had on his arrival in the south, since a nervous James had insisted on added protection. Five hundred soldiers, paid 8d a day, were to guard against 'any tumults and disorder' in Westminster and the Strand.

The king wore a crimson cloak over a velvet coat lined with ermine and a velvet cap. A newly made Imperial Crown was carried before him. Anne, who had also been crowned Queen of Scotland in May 1590, was similarly robed, and, following tradition, had her hair loose about her shoulders and a circlet of gold on her head set with jewels belonging to the late queen.

The service followed 'the forme sett downe in the auncient Booke kept among the Records at Westminster', though for the first time most of the service was in English apart from the Litany, which was in Latin, and the oath, which was in Latin, English and French (the latter due to the ancient royal claim to the French throne). It was also the first time a Scottish king had been crowned on the Stone of Scone, by then fixed into St Edward's Chair, in over 300 years.

Another departure from the usual format was a bit of gay flirting during the homage. James never concealed his fondness for male courtiers, particularly the Duke of Buckingham. One courtier said that 'I never yet saw any fond husband make so much or so great dalliance over his beautiful spouse as I have seen King James over his favourites'. After kneeling before James, another of the king's squeezes, Philip, Earl of Montgomery, gave James a kiss on the cheek and received a playful slap from the newly crowned monarch. The 19-year-old peer, who caught the royal eye through his fondness for hunting and hawking, was one of the new intake of Knights of the

Bath and, rather handily for access to the monarch, was also a gentleman of the privy chamber.

After the coronation, James and Anne retired to Hampton Court before heading west to Winchester and Wilton House to continue their plague avoidance.

The traditional procession from the Tower of London could have been cancelled altogether, but it was such a useful public relations exercise, cementing the alliance between monarch and city, that it was merely postponed until 15 March 1604. The Lord Mayor had budgeted £4,100 for stands and a series of seven wooden arches to line the route towards Westminster. The arches were the work of the joiner Stephen Harrison, and the poets Ben Johnson and Thomas Dekker came up with some of the allegorical themes that each would be based around.

James, Anne and Henry moved to the Tower of London for three days before participating in the spectacle. On the day itself, Dekker noted, 'the streets seemed to be paved with men; stalls instead of rich wares were set out with children; open casements filled up with women'. Many of the houses on the route had 'all glasse windows taken downe, but in their places sparkled so many eyes'. Helping them sparkle was the conduits that normally supplied the streets with fresh water, but which, for one day only, flowed with claret wine.

The procession set off just after 11 a.m. and was much longer than the coronation day one. It consisted of representatives of the court, the judiciary, the civil service and the English aristocracy in order of precedence. James rode a white jennet (a small Spanish horse) beneath a canopy held by eight gentlemen of the privy chamber. Prince Henry followed behind and then the queen carried in a litter. There was music throughout and Latin orations at every one of the seven archways. In Cheapside, the Lord Mayor presented the royal family with cups made of gold as a gesture of loyalty from the city.

All of this would have gladdened the heart of Good Queen Bess, but noticeably failed to move her dour Scottish cousin, as the seventeenth-century historian Arthur Williams noted that, in general, 'the access of the people made him so impatient that he often dispersed them with frowns'. On this day in particular, 'He was not like his predecessor, that with a well-pleased affection met her people's acclamations'. Instead, clearly glad his second coronation celebrations were over, 'he endured the day's brunt with patience being assured he should never have such another'.

CHARLES I
1625–1649

The twenty-four-year reign of Charles I saw a marked deterioration between the court and parliament. In the first years of the reign, he summoned and dissolved parliament three times before, in 1629, beginning an eleven-year period of personal rule. The relationship between monarch and government deteriorated further when, in 1642, attended by soldiers, the king tried to arrest five members of the House of Commons. The Civil War broke out between the Royalists and Parliamentarians, lasting from 1642 until Charles was tried before a tribunal at the end of 1648. He lost by sixty-eight votes to sixty-seven and was executed in Whitehall in January 1649.

Coronations of Charles I, 2 February 1626 and 18 June 1633

Two things spoiled Charles I's coronation – the plague and his wife.

The pestilence that often spread like wildfire through the unhygienic, packed medieval dwellings of pre-Great Fire of London was an ever-present threat. As we have seen, an epidemic had forced James VI & I to reduce the normal celebrations. The 'great dry summer' of 1625 had the same outcome. Although Charles delayed his coronation until 2 February 1626, four days after a thanksgiving service marking the end of the latest outbreak, he still cancelled the usual lavish procession from the Tower to Westminster to be on the safe side.

The arrival of his new young wife, Henrietta Maria of France, was one invasion that was not going to fade away as

Charles I and his consort Henrietta Maria painted by Van Dyck. The queen is offering her husband a garland of laurel, which represents victory. The royal regalia – crown, sceptre and orb – can be seen on the table next to the king.

easily. Though she was pronounced queen on 25 June 1625, she was never crowned or anointed as the king's consort. The problem was that the French princess was uncompromisingly Roman Catholic at a time when Charles's subjects still had the memory of Bloody Mary's harsh regime as a distant but not forgotten memory.

Marriage negotiations had been going in fits and starts for some time. The pope at first refused to grant a dispensation for her to marry the Anglican Charles. To placate His Holiness, as well as his bride to be's brother, King Louis XIII of France, Charles promised to secretly allow English Roman Catholics the right to worship. He also bent over backwards to accommodate Henrietta Maria's religious wishes. He accepted that nothing would stop her worshipping her faith and even agreed that their children's education would be entrusted to her until they were 13 years old. He would make sure she had her own chapel and chaplain at each royal residence, and he allowed her to bring with her from France her own bishop and twenty-eight priests, while making it clear all her attendants could be both French and Catholic.

That sorted out, there was just the wedding to arrange. The first one took place on a platform outside Notre-Dame Cathedral on May Day 1625. It was by proxy, so the Duc de Chevreuse stood in for Charles and Cardinal Richelieu conducted the service. Henrietta Maria wore a bridal gown of silver and gold with a diadem on her head. Her train was so heavy that the three ladies tasked with carrying it couldn't lift it off the ground and a he-man courtier had to walk underneath it, bearing the brunt of the load on his head.

The king's favourite, the Duke of Buckingham, travelled to France to escort the 15-year-old bride across the Channel. Charles was there to meet her at Dover on 11 June and was wreathed with smiles, though slightly concerned about her height. He was, after all, one of our most diminutive monarchs, with his height given at anything between 4ft 8in (142cm) and 5ft 4in (162.5cm). Seeing his concern, she lifted her dress to show she wasn't using any lifts and reassured him: 'Sir I stand upon my own feet; I have no help by art; thus high am I; neither higher nor lower.'

If only she could always have been that accommodating. She initially refused to learn any English (presumably the above quote was originally in French). She also objected to the admittedly odd habit of allowing visitors to the court to watch the royal family eat. One voyeur later wrote: 'Divers of us being at Whitehall to see her being at dinner and the room somewhat overheated with a fire and company, she drove us all out of the chamber. I suppose none but a Queen could have cast such a scowl.' Charles hoped it was just a phase, since, on her sixteenth birthday in December, he told Buckingham he thought his queen was 'mending her manners'.

Meanwhile, plans for the coronation were beginning in earnest. Hoping to placate his prickly bride, Charles decided to hold it on 2 February, Candlemas Day, which is also called the Purification of St Mary the Virgin. Henrietta Maria's anglicised name 'Queen Mary' is included in the documents relating to the coronation. A place was prepared for her in the abbey so she could watch the service without taking part in it. There was a precedent for a consort not fully taking part in a coronation: Charles's mother Anne of Denmark refused to take the sacrament at James VI & I's coronation, complaining that she had already changed from Lutheran to Presbyterian when she married him and became Queen Consort of Scotland, and she wasn't about to change again now he had come south of the border.

The order of service prepared for William Laud, a friend of Buckingham's and later Archbishop of Canterbury, lists her presence on the day and mentions her being crowned. At some point just before the ceremony, however, she pulled out, refusing to attend, much to the king's annoyance. It is unclear when she made the decision. Certainly she was fine with the Protestant clergy on her arrival in England, allowing Laud and the others to kiss her hand.

It appears that it was her spiritual advisor, the young Bishop of Mende, who threw the spanner in the works by declaring she couldn't be allowed to receive her crown from a Church of England priest. Louis XIII backed his sister, writing to Charles that if she took the crown, it must not prejudice her conscience and that a heavenly crown was better.

So Charles was crowned alone, a solitary figure in white walking along the carpeted route from Westminster Hall to the abbey, while his wife watched from a window in Sir Abraham William's apartment in Old Palace Yard, where it was noted her ladies, somewhat tactlessly, could be seen frisking and dancing in the room behind her.

The service was conducted by George Abbot, Archbishop of Canterbury, a forlorn figure who had suffered from severe depression for the past five years, having accidentally shot one of his keepers with his crossbow when out hunting. As his biographer Gustavus Paine notes, Abbot was the 'only translator of the 1611 Bible and the only Archbishop of Canterbury to ever kill a human being'.

History was made, since Charles was the last monarch to be crowned with the existing regalia, including the St Edward's Crown, which would all be melted down and sold off by Parliamentarians following the English Civil War and his own execution, which was a thought unlikely to have entered anyone's head that winter's day.

As usual, there were a couple of incidents that were later commented on. The Duke of Buckingham, for whom Charles revived the ancient title of Lord High Constable, was escorting the king up the steps to the throne when Charles stumbled. Buckingham grabbed the king, at which point Charles removed his hand and, putting it under Buckingham's own arm, said with a smile, 'I have as much need to help you as you to assist me.' There was another awkward moment when the newly crowned sovereign was presented to the assembled congregation by the Earl of Arundel. Instead of a shout of acclamation, there was total silence, until Arundel told them what to do, and his fellow peers, better late than never, shouted out: 'God Save King Charles!'

Religion was another sticking point at Charles's Scottish coronation at Holyrood Chapel on 18 June 1633. The Scots were insulted that it had taken Charles eight years to return to the land of his birth to be acclaimed as king. They were also upset that he brought with him bishops in robes and clergy in white vestments, who genuflected to the altar and were about as High Church as it was possible for an Anglican to be. Even more annoyingly, Charles expected his over-taxed Scottish subjects to pay for the coronation as well for the new parliament building he approved plans for.

At least Henrietta Maria and her Catholic acolytes didn't accompany him to Scotland, as she had the useful excuse that she was pregnant (with the future James II). The couple would frequently come to blows about her religious faith. Hearing that one of her courtiers refused to attend a Protestant ceremony in a royal chapel, Charles exploded with rage: 'If he will not come to my prayers, let him get out of my house!' Another time, when one of her many priests was heard to moan that the queen's closet they were given to use was too small, the king, completely losing the plot, was heard to yell that if the closet was too small, they could use 'the Great Chamber, and if the Great Chamber were not wide enough, they might use the Garden, and if the Garden would not serve them, then was the Park the fittest place!'

CHARLES II
1660–1685

As a boy of 12, Charles had been present at the Battle of Edgehill with his father at the start of the Civil War. He later escaped to France, returning to Scotland in 1650, where he was proclaimed king. Backed by a Scottish army of 10,000 men, he invaded England the following year before being defeated by Cromwell's troops and fleeing again to France. He returned on his thirtieth birthday, 29 May 1660. He agreed to work with parliament, witnessed a cultural revival, particularly in London, and had over a dozen mistresses, including the legendary Nell Gwynne. His reign also saw two significant historical events: the Great Plague of 1665 and the Great Fire of London the following year.

Coronations of Charles II, 1 January 1651 and 23 April 1661

Charles II was crowned twice: firstly at Scone, the traditional site of Scottish coronations, on New Year's Day 1651; and secondly on 23 April 1661, after his triumphant return to London on his thirtieth birthday the year before.

'The Merry Monarch's' coronation is significant for several reasons. It was the last one to feature a procession from the Tower of London to Westminster Hall on the eve of the ceremony. It saw the creation of the regalia – much of which will be used at the coronation of Charles III and thereafter – to replace the historic items destroyed by Oliver Cromwell's regime. It also saw the first tiered stands inside Westminster

Charles II in his coronation robes, in a portrait painted by John Michael Wright, shortly after the ceremony. The centuries-old royal regalia had been melted down and sold off by the Parliamentarians, so a new crown, orb and sceptre had to be made. (Incamerastock/ Alamy Stock Photo)

Abbey, which allowed the congregation to have a clearer view of the ceremony, and which meant that the St Edward's Chair no longer needed to be on an elevated dais. Finally, thanks to the diarist Samuel Pepys, who attended both the procession and the service, we have one of the most detailed and entertaining first-hand accounts of a coronation.

Charles was crowned King of Scotland, England, France and Ireland at Scone Palace in Perthshire two years after his father was beheaded in London in January 1649. It was to be the last coronation held on Scottish soil. He had returned from exile in France and The Hague, and hoped the ceremony would be a prelude to reclaiming the rest of Britain from Oliver Cromwell's Puritan rule.

Charles travelled to Scone on 31 December and the following morning dressed in a robe, which was carried by train-bearers who were sons of royalist aristocrats. They walked in a procession, beneath a canopy of crimson velvet, to the chapel at Moot Hill, where his throne and the Honours of Scotland awaited him atop a 4ft-high (1.2m) dais.

He had to listen to an hour-long sermon given by Robert Douglas, Moderator of the General Assembly, who declared that it was the king's duty to preserve the established religion of Scotland. Just in case Charles didn't get the message, Douglas added the dire warning: 'A king when he getteth his Crown on his head, should think at best, it is but a fading crown.' The crown, faded or not, was placed on the 20-year-old's head, not by a cleric but by an aristocrat, John Campbell, 1st Earl of Loudon, the Scottish Lord Chancellor.

After the service there was a lavish banquet in Scone Palace, which included ten calves' heads and twenty-two salmon. Guests at Charles's table found damask linen napkins embroidered in readiness with his 'CR' cypher.

It would be another nine years before the monarchy was restored and Charles shrewdly chose his thirtieth birthday – 29 May 1660 – for his ceremonial arrival in London. There was then a delay of eleven months before the king was crowned in Westminster Abbey, partly because the regalia and vestments used by previous monarchs during the ceremony had been destroyed under Cromwell's regime. (The jewels were either sold off or melted down, though the silver gilt Coronation Spoon was sold off privately and returned to the Royal

Collection after the Restoration and has been used during the anointing ceremony ever since.)

The man tasked with organising the coronation was Sir Edward Walker, clerk of the Privy Council, who at the time was Charles's right-hand man, having served him loyally throughout his eleven-year exile on the Continent. A coronation committee was convened on 22 October 1650.

One of its tasks was to decide on the replacement regalia. Sir Robert Vyner (or Viner), the Royal Goldsmith from 1660 to 1688, was the man responsible for creating the new items that today still form the central components of the Crown Jewels. Two crowns were to be made for the ceremony. St Edward's Crown, with its solid gold frame, has been used at every coronation since 1661 and was so heavy that for 200 years, from the coronation of Queen Anne in 1702, it was carried in the coronation procession but not worn. In 1911 its weight was reduced to 2.23kg (nearly 5lb) for the coronation of George V. At the same time, it was fitted with permanent semi-precious stones as previously jewels were hired to fit it at each coronation. A second 'Imperiall Crowne', worn at key events such as the State Opening of Parliament, was also designed by Vyner, though it is not the one used today. This contained 890 diamonds, 10 rubies, 18 sapphires, 20 emeralds and 549 pearls. The goldsmith also created two sceptres and the Sovereign's Orb (or 'the Ball with the Crosse', as it is referred to in a contemporary account). The bill for the new regalia came to an eye-watering £12,184 7s 6d (over an estimated £1.8 million at today's rate, using the Bank of England inflation calculator).

Preparing the processional route from the Tower of London to Westminster came under the direction of 'Mr Peter Mills', Surveyor of the City. Among many other decorations, he was responsible for creating four enormous arches, two of which hailed Charles as a modern Caesar Augustus, restoring peace and prosperity to England. The writer John Evelyn thought these structures were 'of good invention and architecture'. His fellow diarist Samuel Pepys, journeying through the city a fortnight before the festivities, 'saw in what forwardness all things are for the Coronacion which will be very magnificent'.

On 22 April, Charles and his younger brother James, Duke of York, arrived at the Tower of London at about 7 a.m. and were met by peers of the realm in preparation for the day's pageantry. The procession formed up at 8 a.m. on Tower Hill, with participants having been told to make sure their horses were 'not unruly or stinking'.

The royal procession set off at 10 a.m., passing houses en route draped with decorative carpets and tapestries. For those watching, fuelled with red or white wine from the conduits, it was a never-ending spectacle, as 1,000 participants rode by on horseback with thousands more on foot. Two hundred musicians took part in twenty-eight musical and two vocal groups. The enthusiastic cacophony of sound led to an unfortunate moment when Charles had to silence the trumpeters after one of their periodic blasts spooked the Duke of York's horse, who bolted, chucking James on to the ground.

Samuel Pepys, in his velvet coat, 'the first day that I put it on, though made half a year ago', watched the procession from Mr Young's, the flag-maker, in Cornhill, where 'we had a good room to ourselves, with wine and good cake and saw the show very well. In which it is impossible to relate the glory of this day.'

The diarist thought, 'The King, in a most rich embroidered suit and cloak, looked most noble', and he was thrilled to note that both Charles 'and the Duke of York took notice of us, as he saw us at the window'.

It wasn't just the royal brothers that caught his eye. There was also the sight of 'ladies out of the windows, one of which over against us I took much notice of, and spoke of her, which made good sport among us'.

Pepys was back the next day to give us an update on the royal proceedings, from his seat in the abbey, where he waited from 4 a.m. until the King's arrival seven hours later.

It was the most extravagant coronation since that of Elizabeth I and Pepys thought what 'a great pleasure it was to see the Abbey raised in the middle, all covered with red, and a throne (that is a chair) and footstool on the top of it; and all the officers of all kinds, so much as the very fidlers, in red vests'.

After the procession of clergy came the Duke of York 'and the King with a scepter (carried by my Lord Sandwich) and sword and mond [the orb] before him, and the crown too. The King in his robes, bare-headed, which was very fine.'

A highlight was witnessing 'The crown being put upon his head', when 'a great shout begun, and he came forth to the throne, and there passed more ceremonies'. Unsurprisingly, given his seven-hour wait, Pepys had to nip out before the last fanfare sounded as 'I had so great a list to piss, that I went out a little while before the King had done all his ceremonies'.

The omnipresent diarist next pops into Westminster Hall, which, thanks to non-existent security, he could just walk into: 'went round the Abbey to Westminster Hall, all the way within rails, and 10,000 people, with the ground covered with blue cloth – and scaffolds all the way.' He was keen to witness what was, after all, a historic occasion, as the last such banquet was in 1559, after Elizabeth I's coronation. What may have struck him, though he fails to mention it, is that it was here only twelve years earlier that the king's father, Charles I, had been tried for his life.

'Into the Hall I got – where it was very fine with hangings and scaffolds one upon another full of brave ladies; and my wife in one little one, on the right hand.' But while Mrs Pepys clung to the scaffolding for a good view, Samuel:

stayed walking up and down, and at last upon one of the side stalls I stood and saw the King come in with all the persons (but the soldiers) that were yesterday in the cavalcade; and a most pleasant sight it was to see them in their several robes.* And the King came in with his crown on, and his sceptre in his hand – under a canopy borne up by six silver staves, carried by Barons of the Cinque Ports – and little bells at every end.

After witnessing the king being served his first course by the Knights of the Bath, and managing to avoid 'these three Lords, Northumberland and Suffolk and the Duke of Ormond, coming before the courses on horseback, and staying so all dinner-time', he witnessed 'Dymock the King's champion, all in armor on horseback, with his spear and target carried before him'. After the champion made the traditional challenge to anyone who dared deny that Charles was the lawful king to mortal combat, 'the King drinks to him, and then sends him the cup which is of gold, and he drinks it off, and then rides back again with the cup in his hand'.

Pepys enjoyed listening to 'the music of all sorts; but above all, the 24 violins' before the king left after 6 p.m. Having been good weather for the last two days of celebration, it waited until:

the King gone out of the Hall; and then it fell a-raining and thundering and lightening as I have not seen it do

---

* The king's elaborate dress, including breeches and stockings, were made of crimson satin. Curiously, rather than being recycled or sent to a museum, these special designs, together with those of the Duke of York, were donated to a theatre. In 1664 the actor Owen Tudor, playing Henry V in the new play by the Earl of Orrery, walked on stage wearing Charles II's coronation suit, giving an interesting historical slant to the role.

for some years – which people did take great notice of; God's blessing of the work of these two days – which is a foolery to take too much notice of such things.

Before leaving, Pepys witnessed a spat between the barons of the Cinque Ports and the king's footmen. The former traditionally carried the canopy above the monarch's head during the processions and then had the perquisite of being allowed to tear it to shreds and sell off pieces. After the royal party there was an unseemly tussle as the footmen snatched the canopy and then the barons tried to grab it back, 'but could not do it till my Lord Duke of Albemarle caused it to be put into Sir R. Pye's hand till tomorrow to be decided'.

Pepys's coronation celebrations ended with a bonfire party at Axe Yard, just south of modern-day Downing Street, where he and his wife drank 'the King's health upon our knees' thanks to the largesse of another guest, Mr Thornbury, yeoman of the wine cellar to the king, who provided the celebratory booze. The diarist recalls, 'we drank the King's health, and nothing else, till one of the gentlemen fell down stark drunk, and there lay spewing'. He too ended up in a bit of a state, when 'my head began to hum, and I to vomit' and, after he crashed out, 'I waked [and] found myself wet with my spewing. Thus did the day end with joy everywhere.' There wasn't much joy the next day when he 'waked in the morning with my head in a sad taking through the last night's drink, which I am very sorry for'.

JAMES II
1685–1688

Like his older brother, James II fled to France during the Civil War. His short reign of three years was dominated by the conflict his firm Roman Catholic beliefs had on his Protestant subjects. Six months into his reign, a rebellion led by Charles II's illegitimate son, the Duke of Monmouth, unsuccessfully tried to oust James. Monmouth was executed and the 'Bloody Assizes' of Judge Jeffries led to a further 230 executions, as well as hundreds of other imprisonments or transportations for life. James became a hate figure as religious persecution grew. The birth of a Roman Catholic male heir to his second wife, Mary of Modena, sounded the death bell for his reign, and parliament invited the king's Protestant daughter, Mary, and her husband, William of Orange, to spearhead the Glorious Revolution.

Coronation of James II, 23 April 1687

The coronation of James II was the last time in British history that a fervent Roman Catholic monarch was crowned at Westminster Abbey. His challenge was how to adapt the traditional service used by his brother, father and grandfather to suit his own conscience. He also sneakily had himself and his consort, Mary of Modena, crowned and anointed according to Catholic rites the day before.

James, Duke of York, converted to Catholicism in 1668 or 1669, when he was in his mid-thirties, influenced by his first wife Anne Hyde, who had changed faith nearly a decade earlier. York did, however, continue to attend Protestant services until 1676. The problem for the House of Stuart came three years earlier when, following Anne's death, James married Mary of Modena, a 15-year-old Italian princess, by proxy in a Roman Catholic ceremony. When she arrived in England she was treated with suspicion by the public even though the couple married again in a brief Anglican ceremony.

With James's older brother Charles II having no legitimate heir, the throne would be inherited by a Catholic couple who, in all likelihood, would have a son born into that faith, who would displace James's two daughters by Anne Hyde, Mary and Anne. King Charles II opposed this crisis of faith within the royal family and ordered that these two nieces should be brought up in the Anglican faith; he also supported the marriage between Mary and her cousin, the Protestant William of Orange. James, however, remained a staunch adherent to the Church of Rome. He once claimed, 'If occasion were, I hope God would give me his grace to suffer death for the true Catholic religion as well as banishment.'

This firm belief sparked what became known as the Exclusion Crisis. Titus Oates, a defrocked Anglican cleric, spoke of a 'Popish plot' to kill Charles and replace him with James as monarch. Predictably it led to a wave of anti-Catholic feeling in the country, and prompted the Earl of Shaftesbury, a founder of the Whig Party, to propose an Exclusion Bill to bar James from the throne. Some MPs even wanted Charles's illegitimate son, the Duke of Monmouth, to succeed him as king. Then, just as the bill could have been passed, Charles, in order to protect the current line of succession, dissolved parliament in 1679 and then again in 1680 and '81. James took a more backseat role in Charles's political affairs and in 1680 headed to Edinburgh to become the Lord High Commissioner of Scotland.

Things looked up for the duke when the Rye House Plot of 1683 threatened to mount an insurrection or even an assassination attempt against the king and his brother, and replace the monarchy with a Cromwellian-style commonwealth. Just as Queen Victoria's many assassination attempts saw an upsurge in popularity for the monarchy, so the alienated James was restored in the public's favour and once again became a privy councillor.

On Monday 2 February 1685, Charles II had a stroke and, after suffering further convulsions, died four days later. James stayed by his brother's bedside throughout the ordeal and even engineered a deathbed religious conversion for the king. He asked Charles if he would like to receive unction from a Roman Catholic priest and the king eagerly whispered, 'For God's sake brother do, and please lose no time.' James managed to arrange for Father Huddleston, a Benedictine monk, to perform this final anointing. It must have been an emotional moment for all concerned since Huddleston had assisted Charles to escape to France thirty-four years earlier following the Battle of Worcester.

James called a meeting of the Privy Council later the same day. He no longer had to acquiesce to his brother's wishes and made it clear he would remain an adherent to the Roman Catholic faith. He did, however, claim that he realised the importance of the Church of England to the monarchy and that he would therefore 'always take care to defend and support'. So relieved were the privy councillors with this conciliatory approach that they had his impromptu speech printed and circulated. The new king did, however, avoid saying he would 'defend' the Church of England when he addressed his first parliament. Instead, he said that the Anglican clergy 'had showed themselves so eminently loyal in the worst of times' and that he expected them to support the monarchy.

He left no one in doubt about his own loyalty to his faith when, on the first Sunday of his reign, he openly attended Mass in the

Queen's Chapel in St James's Palace. He also held Charles II's funeral privately – 'very obscurely', sniffed the Protestant diarist John Evelyn – on 14 February. James made it clear that, when it came to his coronation, no rites were to be used that were contrary to his own beliefs. Even so, he intended for it to be a truly memorable day. The Anglo-Irish herald and genealogist Francis Sandford, who produced the definitive *History of the Coronation of the most high, most mighty, and most excellent monarch, James II …*, made the new king's wishes known. He states James wanted 'All that Art, Ornament and Expence could do to the making of the Spectacle Dazzling and Stupendious'. This does not quite ring true with the king's request to the coronation committee 'to consider how low the prices might be reduced'. In the end, the works side of the ceremony cost £1,181 and the 'Great Wardrobe' covering all the various robes and materials for the event came to £4,553. Both these amounts were cheaper than the equivalents for the other late Stuart coronations of Charles II, William and Mary, and Anne.

One significant omission was the abandonment of the traditional procession from the Tower of London to Westminster. Given the public's volatile relationship with James over the past few years, it was probably a wise move, although the London citizens seemed to have loved a good coronation pageant or two, and the almost biblical turning of water into wine at the city's conduits was always an added bonus.

In regard to the service itself, William Sancroft, Archbishop of Canterbury, and six bishops reviewed the traditional service, which was shortened and omitted the communion. In addition, many traditional prayers were dropped, and the litany was moved from after the royal oath to before it.

On the morning of the coronation, James and Mary travelled to Westminster Hall from Whitehall Palace, joining the assembled nobles at eleven o'clock. They sat on their twin thrones while the ceremonial swords and golden spurs were laid on the table before them. Then the dean arrived with the crown and other regalia, which were also laid before the king and consort before being handed to the peers tasked to carry them to the abbey.

The procession then formed, led by drummers and trumpeters, city aldermen, masters of chancery, gentlemen of the privy chamber, judges, choristers from the King's Chapel as well as from Westminster Abbey and then the peers of the realm in reverse order of importance, from barons to dukes.

There then followed Mary of Modena's procession, with the Duke of Beaufort carrying her crown. This is probably her coronation crown, which no longer exists. It was made by the jeweller Richard Beauvoir, who also made her State Crown and her diadem, which are both still part of the Crown Jewels. The State Crown is gold framed with four half-arches each set with a central row of pearls. Today, rock crystals replace the diamonds, which were hired for this and subsequent coronations of Mary II, Queen Anne and Queen Caroline.

James's procession followed and, like the queen, he walked beneath a canopy carried by sixteen Cinque Port barons, four carrying each of the staves. Both members of the royal couple wore robes furred with ermine and, while the king wore a velvet cap on his head, the queen wore a gold circlet. The king's crown was carried by the Duke of Ormonde.

The couple walked on a blue carpet to the abbey with, according to the *London Gazette*, 'the whole passage being railed in and guarded with His Majesty's horse and foot guards'.

Inside the abbey, the couple ascended the steps of the coronation theatre in their chairs of state before the recognition, after which they walked to the High Altar, where the regalia was presented. The moment of crowning James took place at 'just three of the clock in the afternoon', which unleashed a cacophony of sound: 'All the people shouted, the Drums and Trumpets sounded, and the guns in St James's Park, and great guns at the Tower were discharged and all the peers put on their coronets.'

John Evelyn, who was not present, wrote there was '(to the great sorrow of the people) no Sacrament, as ought to have been'. Indeed, this took place the previous day at Whitehall Palace, where the king was crowned and took communion according to the Roman Catholic rite.

After Mary's crowning the couple moved to St Edward's Chapel, where they changed into robes of purple velvet prior to walking back to Westminster Hall.

The day had not gone without the occasional mishap. The crown slipped on James's head as it was being placed by the archbishop, which was seen as a bad omen, as was the moment when the royal standard flying from the Tower of London was torn off by the wind.

James reduced the coronation banquet from three courses, enjoyed in Charles II's day, to two. Even so, it seems to have been lavish with £1,210 spent on 1,445 dishes, of which 175 were served at the royal table, supplying everything from 'stags tongues' and 'Bolonia sausage' to 'Ragou of Oysters' and 'Blumange'.

The royal couple left for Whitehall at 7 p.m. That evening's coronation firework display was postponed 'by reason of the great Fatigue of the Day'. James and Mary watched it the following evening from the roof of Whitehall Palace. It lasted forty-five minutes and consisted of the allegorical figures of Pater Patriae (the father of the country) and Monarchia (the monarchy) with a central monogram of James II, with a sun symbol hovering above it, reminiscent of Louis XIV's 'le Roi Soleil'.

Increasingly, the coronation celebrations were starting to be wide-ranging and not just confined to London. In Bristol, for instance, where the four conduits *did* run with wine, we are told: 'The Concourse of People as well as Citizens as from the

Country was the greatest that has been known, and most part of the Night was spent with Bonfires, Ringing of Bells and all the demonstrations of a general satisfaction.'

WILLIAM III
1689–1702
AND MARY II
1689–1694

William III, also known as William of Orange, was Stadtholder (head of state) of the Dutch Republic from 1672. In 1677 he married his first cousin Mary, the eldest daughter of his maternal uncle James, Duke of York, later James II. In 1689 they succeeded the deposed James, though the following year an invasion of Ireland by James had to be put down by William at the Battle of the Boyne, which is still commemorated by unionists in Ulster. William remained a champion of the Protestant faith and participated in several wars against the Catholic Louis XIV of France. Mary died in 1694 and William ruled alone until 1702. The couple had no children and the king was succeeded by Mary's younger sister, Anne.

Coronation of William III and Mary II, 11 April 1689

James II's three-year reign grew increasingly unpopular with the Protestant majority, who feared a revival of Catholicism,

Parliament is seen offering the crown to William and Mary in 1689 after the expulsion of Mary's deeply unpopular Catholic father James II. The fervently Protestant couple would rule jointly until Mary's death in 1694. (Wellcome Collection)

particularly following the birth of his son James Frances Edward Stuart, who was baptised a Roman Catholic. On 30 June 1688, a group of political figures comprising six peers and a senior bishop, later dubbed the 'immortal seven', invited William to try to persuade his father-in-law King James to recognise his elder daughter – William's Protestant wife Mary – as his heir. In what would become known as the Glorious Revolution, William landed at Brixham in Devon on 5 November 1688 with 40,000 men aboard 463 ships, a force greater than the Spanish Armada of 1588. Shortly afterwards James was deposed and exiled to France.

Mary only arrived in England on 11 February 1689, where she was reunited, in floods of tears, with William. Two days later, the couple appeared at Banqueting House in Whitehall to receive a delegation from parliament, who read out the Declaration of Rights to them. Although Mary had the stronger claim to the throne as the elder daughter of James, William refused the position of consort and it had already been decided that the couple should reign as joint sovereigns. It was, however, made clear that the power would 'be only in and executed by the said Prince of Orange' in both their names. At the meeting on the 13th, William agreed, 'we thankfully accept what you have offered us', and promised to rule according to law and the parliament. In December, the declaration was enshrined in law as the Bill of Rights, which has since become one of the cornerstones of British democracy.

While the thoughts of parliament turned to publicly honouring the co-rulers with a suitable coronation, Mary's chief concern that spring was the king's ill-health. The polluted London air from thousands of smoky coal fires had exacerbated his chronic asthma. It was made worse by having to attend malodorous, packed court functions illuminated by hundreds of candles, which further worsened the indoor air quality. In February 1689, he had moved to Hampton Court, but his health failed to improve and, worryingly, he started to cough up blood. Later that year, having struggled through his coronation ceremony, William decided to purchase Kensington House, owned by Lord Nottingham, which was then in the countryside just outside London. He transformed much of it into the palace we know today and his statue, facing the Golden Gates, dominates the view of the south side of 'KP'.

The coronation was fixed for 11 April 1689, which broke with tradition by not being either a major saint's day or a Sunday. The day got off to rather an awkward start. The news came through that, far from acquiescing to his exile, James II had landed in Ireland with a French army. A letter arrived at Whitehall Palace addressed to Mary from her irate father, which made clear what he thought of his daughter usurping his throne. 'Your being crowned is in your own power,' he fumed, 'if you do it while I and the Prince of Wales are living, the curses of an angry father will fall on you, as well as those of a God who commands obedience to parents.' Mary was dressing for the ceremony when the letter arrived and it is unclear if she knew of the contents as it was intercepted by Lord Nottingham. Certainly, she made no reference to it in her journal account of the day's events. It was William who eventually replied to his father-in-law, telling him in no uncertain terms that 'all he [William] had done was with his wife's advice and approbation'.

The royal couple departed Whitehall Palace by barge for the short river journey to the Palace of Westminster, where they were met by peers in ermine-edged robes of state. Only eighty-one members of the aristocracy out of 153 invited, as well as only ten bishops, turned up, suggesting the absentees were either indifferent or not in favour of replacing a king who had been crowned and anointed only four years earlier.

One who definitely felt he was bound to his oath of allegiance to James II was William Sancroft, the seventy-ninth Archbishop of Canterbury, who refused to officiate and so was replaced the following year. The co-rulers were therefore crowned by Dr Henry Compton, the Bishop of London. Compton was not only a teacher to the young Princess Mary and her sister Anne, he was also one of the 'Immortal Seven' – six peers and a bishop – who, strongly opposed to James, had written to William in June 1688 urging him to use military force to replace the king with the Protestant Mary.

After three hours at Westminster, William and Mary walked together in procession to the abbey. To emphasise their joint role, they both wore crimson velvet robes, while William wore a velvet cap and Mary wore the diadem made

for her stepmother Queen Mary of Modena. They also processed side by side under the same canopy supported by the
Cinque Port knights.

Inside the abbey, they both received the Sword of State, as
well as a copy of the Bible each, and the spurs and orb. While
William was crowned with St Edward's Crown, Mary was
crowned with Mary of Modena's State Crown. According to
the following week's *London Gazette*, at the moment of crowning at four o'clock, 'the sight whereof the people shouted, the
drums and trumpets sounded, the great guns were discharged,
and the peers and peeresses put on their coronets.'

As well as being crowned at the same moment, they were also
anointed together by the bishop. Given that William, still suffering from the after-effects of his asthma attack, arrived looking
like death warmed up, it didn't help that he had to prostrate
himself with his shirt undone to the waist to receive the holy
oil. A new piece of royal regalia had to be made for Mary: a
sceptre with a dove. Since Mary was queen in her own right, the
dove has spread wings, unlike the dove on the queen consort's
sceptre, which has folded wings. It has never been used since the
1689 coronation, since the later queens regnant – Anne, Victoria
and Elizabeth II – all used the sovereign's sceptre.

Although Mary, as the daughter of James II, had the greater
claim to the throne, it was William who was crowned seated
in St Edward's Chair. A chair, virtually alike in design, was
therefore created for Mary. This 'Mary II Chair' or 'Marian
Chair' was commissioned and paid for by the government
and, like the St Edward's Chair, was covered in cloth of gold
on the day. It is made of oak, stained dark brown and it too
has four lions decorating its legs. Like its companion, it suffered greatly from the Westminster school graffiti artists, who
scratched their names and dates across it – 'G. Dush 1759',
'Greville 1786', 'M Harker, 1792' etc. In his book on the history

of the Coronation Chair, Warwick Rodwell writes that Mary's version 'is a simple design. It gives the impression of having been "knocked up" hurriedly and cheaply for the coronation: it is decidedly not a work of high-class joinery.'

Like Mary's sceptre, it was only used on this one occasion, although in recent years it has been restored and now has pride of place in the abbey's Queen's Diamond Jubilee Galleries.

Given that William and Mary owed their positions to the will of parliament, the traditional oath had to be rewritten. Instead of swearing to uphold the laws of their predecessors, the couple swore to rule 'according to the statutes in Parliament agreed upon and the laws and customs of the same'.

In his sermon, Gilbert Burnet, Bishop of Salisbury, declared, 'may your fleets be prosperous and your armies victorious. But may you soon have cause never to use either.' Given that morning's letter from his warmongering father-in-law, William must have thought, 'some hope!'

As with most British coronations, not everything went to plan. The diamond and ruby ring William presented to Mary, which had been enlarged for the ceremony, was mistakenly jammed on to one of the king's fingers by mistake. Then there was a whispered spat between the two royal sisters. Anne, seeing the evident strain the queen was under, muttered, 'I pity your fatigue, Madam', to which Mary snapped back, 'a crown is not so heavy as it seems!'

There was an unintentionally comic moment when the couple were supposed to make an offering of a roll of silk and twenty pieces of gold to the abbey to mark their coronation. The material was duly placed on the High Altar and then Compton turned to them with a bowl for the much-anticipated coins. William and Mary looked at each other blankly and at Compton with some embarrassment. Either no one had briefed them or they had forgotten to come with the money.

Fortunately, the Earl of Danby (another of the 'Immortal Seven' and who had also arranged the couple's marriage) was able to cough up some coins, even if they weren't twenty in number or golden.

William was, above all, a man of strong religious faith and he looked to the Almighty for support in his new role as monarch of a foreign country: 'It is the hand of God that has so disposed of it. I hope it will be to His glory, but it is no small burden I have to carry.'

That said, the Calvinist King Billy thought the ceremony he had just undertaken was far too ritualistic. He commented to his old friend Nicholas Witsen, Burgomaster of Amsterdam, about 'the comedy of the coronation' and 'those foolish old Popist ceremonies'. Mary was similarly tickled by all the pomp and ceremony, labelling it 'all vanity'.

Despite liberating Britain from the threat of a major Catholic revival under James II, William and Mary didn't feel enamoured with their new life. Mary wrote that she found the first twelve months back in the land of her birth 'a year of trial in every way', adding, 'I still love Holland and I shall always remember the tranquillity I enjoyed there and that I shall never find here.' William was also homesick, exclaiming shortly after the coronation, 'Oh for the wings of a bird! I would give ten thousand pounds to be in Holland now.'

ANNE
1702–1714

The last of the Stuart dynasty, Queen Anne was 37 when she became queen. The death of her heir Prince William, Duke of Gloucester, in 1700, at the age of 11, meant that concern for the succession to the throne dominated her twelve-year rule. Constitutionally, her reign is best remembered for the 1707 Act of Union, which formalised the relationship between Scotland and England, creating Great Britain. The brilliant military leadership of John Churchill, 1st Duke of Marlborough, led to victories at the battles of Blenheim, Ramillies and Oudenarde. Literary giants such as Jonathan Swift, Alexander Pope and Daniel Defoe flourished at this time and Christopher Wren's St Paul's Cathedral was officially declared complete on Christmas Day 1711.

Coronation of Anne, 23 April 1714

Queen Anne was the only monarch to arrive at Westminster Abbey for her coronation on an open sedan chair carried by four Yeomen of the Guard, beneath a canopy. Behind her, over the chair back, billowed her 18ft-long (5.5m) crimson train carried by attendants including the Master of the Robes.

Seventeen pregnancies, resulting in just five live births and only one child   William, Duke of Gloucester, surviving infancy (only to die aged 11) – had taken their toll on Anne's mental and physical well-being. Aged 37 at the time of her coronation, she was semi-disabled, barely able to walk.

Many of her biographers blame her fragility on gout, largely based on contemporary accounts, including the letters of her erstwhile friend Sarah Churchill, Duchess of Marlborough. Some even suggest she drank brandy to excess, which caused her gout. In *The Sickly Stuarts*, Professor Frederick Holmes challenged this point of view, arguing that gout is rare in premenopausal women and the cause of Anne's debilitating health was likely to have been the auto-immune disease lupus, which can cause foetal wastage.

*A 1706 portrait by Charles Boit of Queen Anne with her consort
Prince George of Denmark, the last male consort to take part in a
coronation ceremony until the Duke of Edinburgh in 1953.
(The Picture Art Collection/Alamy Stock Photo)*

Whatever the reason for her disability, Anne managed to
walk from the abbey's Great West Door to the choir and also
to withstand the five-hour ceremony. She arrived at eleven
o'clock and it would be nearly 4 p.m. before the crown was
finally placed on her bewigged head.

The travel writer Celia Fiennes was an eyewitness to the
historic occasion, noting the huge public interest in the coronation, with 'prodigious numbers in scaffolds built in the
Abbey and all the streets on each side to Westminster Hall'. The
person ultimately responsible for the seating was Christopher
Wren, the architect of St Paul's Cathedral, who was appointed

Surveyor of the Fabric at Westminster Abbey in 1698. The Earl Marshal informed Wren that each peer in attendance was to be given eight tickets, so:

> care must be taken to make galleries and seats for as many as possible on each side of the Quire and Great Theatre (and elsewhere convenient). And you may make use of the Crown Arches over the Upper Galleries between the Great Pillars of the Musick Gallery as you did the last Coronation.

It's worth remembering that Wren and his team only had a short time to complete the stands, since William III had died on 8 March 1702 and was buried in the abbey on 12 April, just eleven days before the coronation.

An equal rush, and at a significant expense, was the clothing and jewellery for the queen and her entourage, which came to £8,828. Anne wore a splendid crimson velvet dress above an under-robe of 'gold tissue' with 'very rich embroidery of jewels about it, her petticoat the same gold and silver lace between rows of diamonds embroidered, her linen fine … her head as well dressed with diamonds that brilled and flared'. Also adding a dazzling touch was the Great George of the Order of the Garter, a gold and enamel badge depicting St George on horseback slaying the dragon with a spear.

The purse strings for the queen's appearance were held by her strong-willed formidable favourite Sarah Churchill, who managed to accrue for herself a bevy of court positions including Groom of the Stole, Keeper of the Privy Purse and Mistress of the Robes. Her detailed accounts show that £10 15s were spent for 'dressing Her Majesty's head', with £12 spent on 'a head of hair with long locks and puffs' (i.e., a wig) and 2s 6d spent on 'a pair of favourites' (a 'favourite' being a curl or lock of hair that hung loose on the forehead). Churchill also paid a

Mrs Banks 30s for the petticoat and a Mrs Ducaila for supplying the hair decorations and 72ft (22m) of gold ribbon 'for her
Majesty's head', though it is unclear how, if at all, she wore that.
With her swollen arthritic limbs, it was probably a relief for
Anne to abandon the usual buskins (knee-length boot made of
cloth of gold) and sandals worn by previous monarchs, including the last queen regnant, Elizabeth I.

The sermon was conducted by John Sharp, Archbishop
of York, whom Anne thought more High Church than his
Canterbury counterpart. Sharp was her close confidant and
advisor, and he recorded that she had said 'that I would be
her confessor, and she would be mine'. He promised he'd 'give
as little interruption to it as possible' – perhaps they both had
in mind the sermon given by George Morley, Archbishop of
Canterbury, at her uncle Charles II's coronation, which lasted
an hour and a half. It may also have had something to do with
the fact he was suffering from kidney stones too. Despite its
brevity, the sermon failed to impress Sarah Churchill, who
labelled it 'very dull and heavy'. Poignantly, given that it was
only two years since Anne's final miscarriage, the same year
her son the Duke of Gloucester died, the queen's chosen text
for the sermon came from Isaiah 49:23, 'Kings will be your
foster fathers, and their queens your nursing mothers.'

After the sermon, Anne struggled to her feet for the proclamation by the archbishop: 'Do you take this to be your sovereign
to be over you?' After promising to maintain all the privileges of
Church and state, Anne then received the gold spurs and Sword
of State, masculine symbols of regality that had been given to
William III but not to Mary II, before being presented with the
ring, orb and sceptre, and finally being anointed.

At this point, Thomas Tenison, Archbishop of Canterbury,
had his moment in the sun when he came forward for the
actual crowning, proclaiming her Queen of England, Scotland,

Ireland and France. The nineteenth-century biographer Agnes Strickland thought the inclusion of the last territory, 150 years after Mary I had lost Calais, 'an absurd fiction of national pride'. Following the usual practice, the jewels were on hire, being the same ones used by Anne's stepmother, Mary of Modena, at the 1685 coronation. Nevertheless, one report noted the crown was 'vastly rich in diamonds' and 'fixed on her head with huzzas and sounds of drums, trumpets and guns'. Celia Fiennes added her own downbeat commentary that, 'being only made for this ceremony and pulled to pieces again', the cost was 'only so much for the hire of the such jewels that made it'.

Tenison also expressed the rather tactless hope that the queen would 'leave a numerous posterity to rule these kingdoms', which can't have helped Anne's natural propensity for blushing.

After Anne had tottered to the altar for the sacrament, there came the homage. After the clergy the first to kneel before her was her consort, George of Denmark, in a gesture that would only be repeated once again 250 years later, when the Duke of Edinburgh promised to become the 'liege man of life and limb' to Elizabeth II. Anne had wanted to make George her king consort but had been talked out of it by John Churchill, Duke of Marlborough. Instead, she awarded him the title of Generalissimo of all her forces and later Lord High Admiral of the navy (the latter was an honour Elizabeth II gave to Prince Philip on his ninetieth birthday). The prince was widely ridiculed. Charles II once joked, 'I have tried him drunk, and I have tried him sober, and there in nothing in him.' The Tory politician Lord Mulgrave caustically commented that it was a good job George had asthma, claiming he had to breathe hard in case people mistook him for dead and buried him. Nor did he fare well historically. The next queen regnant, Victoria, thought him 'stupid and insignificant', as most men were when compared to her paragon of men, Prince Albert.

At this point, the anointed and crowned queen withdrew to King Edward's Chapel 'for private prayer' and presumably a comfort break, since listed on the royal accounts were 'two close stools' for Anne's personal use.

The queen emerged wearing a purple train (as did Elizabeth II) instead of a crimson one to signify her newly crowned status. She also wore a different crown of state. She now walked in procession to the Great West Door and her waiting chair, 'obliging looks and bows to all that saluted her and were spectators in the abbey and all the streets'.

Anne was taken in procession to Westminster Hall, where she sat on a throne beneath a canopy. Protocol dictated she should sit in splendid isolation but, on a whim, she beckoned George and had him placed on her left. The second course was led in by the Earl Marshal, the Lord High Steward and the Lord High Chamberlain on horseback, 'and the Cookes came up with their point aprons and towells about their shoulders of point'. Then the Champion also arrived on horseback to throw down the gauntlet to anyone contesting Anne's right to the throne, which, as usual, no one did.

The queen returned to St James's Palace at 8.30 p.m., some nine and a half hours after her arrival at the abbey, presumably exhausted after her ordeal.

One of the perquisites after the coronation was for the abbey authorities to divide the spoils left behind, though they were to be disappointed in Anne's case as she made sure her courtiers left nothing behind. Instead, a few years later, she donated a humongous altarpiece, created by Grinling Gibbons based on a design by Wren, that had been part of Whitehall Palace before the disastrous fire of 1698 destroyed the building. This proved to be a white elephant that various deans of Westminster tried to have reduced or dismantled until it finally bit the dust in preparation for the Coronation of George IV in 1821.

HOUSE OF HANOVER,
1714–1901

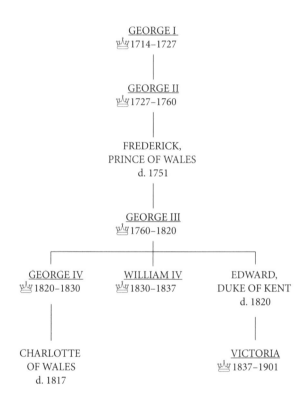

GEORGE I
👑 1714–1727

GEORGE II
👑 1727–1760

FREDERICK,
PRINCE OF WALES
d. 1751

GEORGE III
👑 1760–1820

GEORGE IV
👑 1820–1830

WILLIAM IV
👑 1830–1837

EDWARD,
DUKE OF KENT
d. 1820

CHARLOTTE
OF WALES
d. 1817

VICTORIA
👑 1837–1901

GEORGE I
1714–1727

*George I was the first British monarch of the House of Hanover.
The Stuart dynasty ended with the death of George's second
cousin Queen Anne on 1 August 1714. His reign saw the beginning of Cabinet government led by a prime minister, the first of
whom was Robert Walpole.*

Coronation of George I, 20 October 1714

Under the terms of the 1689 Bill of Rights, Roman Catholics
were barred from succeeding to the throne following the disastrous reign of the papist James II. His successor William III was
childless, while his heir, Anne, had only one child who survived
infancy, only to die aged 11.

The 1701 Act of Settlement legislated that should neither
William nor Anne leave issue, the throne would go the nearest
Protestant relation, Sophia, Electress of Hanover, granddaughter of King James I. In the event, Sophia died two months
before Queen Anne, so it was her son, George Louis, who
succeeded as king. In doing so, the succession bypassed fifty-
five living Roman Catholic descendants of King James, all of
whom would have had a stronger claim than George to the
throne had Catholics not been disqualified.

The chief of these Jacobite claimants, James Francis Edward
Stuart (nicknamed 'the Old Pretender'), son of James II, lived
in Lorraine, closer to Britain than Hanover, and had already
led an unsuccessful invasion across the Channel in 1708.
Despite the ever-present Jacobite threat, George didn't rush

to claim his prize and took a leisurely six weeks to arrive in England, landing on 18 September 1714.

To bolster his claim to the throne, George's coronation was scheduled to take place just over a month later, on 20 October. Such a high-profile event was anathema to the new king, who disliked any formality, crowds of onlookers and the trappings of monarchy. En route to England he had arrived at The Hague at two in the morning to avoid 'much embarrassment and a great crowd of people'. When he eventually reached his new capital, it was again dark and his carriage procession into St James's Palace was barely noticed.

Unsurprisingly, George found the coronation ceremony irksome. For a start, it was a lengthy ordeal, beginning with his arrival at the abbey at 9 a.m. and ending twelve hours later, following a banquet at Westminster Hall. The new king had only a rudimentary grasp of the English language and so much of the service was conducted in Latin. Given the terms of the Act of Settlement, George had to promise 'to joyn in communion with the Church of England as by law established'. The recent 1707 Act of Union with Scotland meant the coronation oath also made sure the king would 'maintain and preserve inviolably the settlement of the Church of Scotland'.

Inevitably there was the odd unplanned incident. Britain's oldest military corps, the Yeomen of the Guard, on ceremonial duty, left their positions and wandered into the coronation theatre, which is the area of the abbey where the crowning takes place. There was a far greater disturbance in the country at large on coronation day, though, with pro-Jacobite riots in twenty locations, including Norwich, Reading, Birmingham, Bristol and Chippenham. These were a precursor to another invasion the following year, known as 'the Fifteen', when the Old Pretender landed in Scotland in an ultimately unsuccessful attempt to seize the throne.

George's coronation cost a relatively modest £7,287. Of this, the significant amount of £1,782 went to one Stephen Toulouze, listed on the audit as 'embroiderer'. A further £80 went on setting some of the Stuart Crown Jewels into a new crown for George. The one made for Charles II and worn by James II, William III and Anne had grown weak and so the main jewels including the Black Prince's 'ruby', and the monde and cross added for James II were reused. A further £1,060 was spent on purchasing 160 new diamonds, 6 emeralds, 2 sapphires and 265 pearls.

Another crown was used during the service. The king's son, George Augustus, Prince of Wales, attended wearing the crown made for James II's consort, Mary of Modena. This very visible gesture was clearly emphasising the strength of the succession in the new regime after the Stuart Charles II, William III and Anne had all died leaving no living legitimate heirs.

Someone who didn't get to wear a crown that October day was Sophia Dorothea, the king's former wife. Years before she had begun an affair with the Swedish Count Philip von Königsmarck. In 1694, shortly after George was tipped off about his wife's infidelity, Königsmarck was murdered and Sophia Dorothea was banished to Ahlden House in Lüneburg Heath, north Germany. The couple were divorced due to her betrayal and for 'maliciously leaving her husband'. This was more than a bit rich of George as, by that fateful year of 1694, he already had two illegitimate children with his mistress Melusine von der Schulenburg who, after his accession to the British throne, accompanied him to London and was ennobled as Duchess of Kendal.

Melusine wasn't the only royal mistress to attend the coronation of George I. Also in attendance were several of her feistier predecessors. When, following tradition, the Archbishop of Canterbury presented the king to all four sides of the abbey, asking the people if they were prepared to recognise him as their sovereign, Lady Dorchester, one of James II's mistresses, loudly retorted: 'Does the old Fool think that anybody will say no with so many drawn swords?' Later on, Lady D caught up with the Duchess of Portsmouth (one of Charles II's surviving squeezes) and Lady Orkney (mistress to William III) and cheerily observed: 'Good God! Who would have thought we three whores would have met together here!'

GEORGE II
1727–1760

Like his father, George II had been born in north Germany and is the most recent British monarch not to have been born in the UK. Also like his father, he spent a considerable amount of time in Hanover, where he could exert more direct control over government affairs than he could in Britain. In 1743 he became the last British monarch to lead troops into battle when he took part in the Battle of Dettingen. Two years later, Charles Edward Stuart (Bonnie Prince Charlie) led an unsuccessful Jacobite rebellion to try to oust George in favour of the Old Pretender, James Stuart.

Coronation of George II, 11 October 1727

The coronation of George II and his consort, Caroline of Ansbach, was far more lavish than that of George I, and it is brilliantly (and acerbically) brought to life in the memoirs of the courtier and political writer Lord John Hervey.

George I, who was Elector of Hanover before succeeding to the British throne, died en route to the electorate on 11 June 1727. At Delden, near the Dutch border, the king stopped for supper and is said to have overindulged on watermelon. Soon afterwards someone is supposed to have thrown a letter from his late ex-wife Sophia Dorothea, whom he had abandoned, into his carriage – a reminder of the worrying prophecy that he would not survive her by a year. Either the watermelons or the letter (or both) finished him off. The king suffered a stroke and died before his carriage reached Osnabrück.

His heir George Augustus, and his wife Caroline, were enjoying an afternoon nap at their home, Richmond Lodge, when Robert Walpole, First Lord of the Treasury, arrived to tell them the king was dead. In a moment of farce, the Prince of Wales was buttoning up his breeches when he learned he was the new King George II.

The younger George determined his coronation would be more lavish than his father's had been, as John Hervey, the royal vice chamberlain, recorded: 'The present King differing so much from the last, that all the pageantry and splendour, badges and trappings of royalty, were as pleasing to the son as they were irksome to the father.'

On the day of their coronation, the king and queen arrived at Westminster Hall before 9 a.m. The Holy Bible and the regalia were brought from the abbey and, shortly before noon, the royal procession formed up along a raised wooden platform, covered in blue cloth with rails on either side. It was led by the King's Herb Woman and her team, who scented the path with herbs ahead of the vast snaking procession of civic dignitaries, clergy, Knights of the Bath and courtiers, before the king, in all his majesty, preceded by Queen Caroline in all hers.

George was dressed in crimson velvet robes trimmed with ermine and bordered by gold lace. Still uncrowned, he wore a cap of estate in crimson velvet adorned with large jewels.

According to that week's *London Gazette*, William Wake, Archbishop of Canterbury, 'put the crown reverently upon his Majesty's Head, at which sight all the Spectators repeated their loud Shouts, the Trumpets Sounded and upon a Signal given, the great Guns in the Park and in the Tower were shot off'.

The queen was dressed in purple robes furred with ermine and, on her head, she wore a circle of gold set with large jewels. In fact, she quite possibly held the record for being the most bejewelled queen consort in a millennium of coronations. She wore so much that she sweated profusely and breathed hard under all the weight, and noticeably clanked her way through the abbey assisted by her daughters, the princesses Anne, Amelia and Caroline, carrying her train. It was estimated she wore several million pounds' worth of gems, most of them hired, as Hervey couldn't fail to notice:

> besides her own jewels (which were a great number and very valuable) she had on her head and on her shoulders all the pearls she could borrow off the ladies of quality at one end of town, and on her petticoat all the diamonds she could hire off the Jews and jewellers at the other.

Hervey caustically refers to this Christmas tree effect as a 'mixture of magnificence and meanness'. So encrusted was the queen's dress that a special pulley was devised to lift the royal skirt when its occupant needed to kneel in prayer at various points during the ceremony.

One of the reasons for Caroline having to hire this treasure trove was that, when her father-in-law succeeded to the throne, he distributed much of Queen Anne's collection to his mistress Melusine von der Schulenburg and his half-sister Sophia von Kielmansegg. Hervey recorded, 'Lady Suffolk told me Queen Caroline never obtained of the late Queen's jewels but one pearl necklace.'

Interestingly, this surviving Stuart necklace, together with one belonging to Caroline, was given to Elizabeth II as a wedding present by her parents in 1947 and became one of her favourite pieces. The late queen always wore them together as one double-strand necklace. Queen Anne's, made up of forty-six pearls, is the smaller, while Caroline's has fifty pearls. As Princess Elizabeth, she wore them for her wedding to Lt Philip Mountbatten. As she was getting ready to leave, it was remembered that the pearls were on display with her other presents at St James's Palace and her private secretary, John Colville, had to dash down the Mall to retrieve them.

Adding to the majesty of George's coronation service was the music of George Frideric Handel, who had been commissioned to write four new anthems for the coronation, including 'Zadok the Priest', which has since become an integral part of the ceremony.

One member of the royal family not there to hear it was the king's eldest son, Frederick, Prince of Wales. The Hanoverian monarchs famously disliked their heirs and vice versa. Frederick was pointedly not invited to the London ceremony and had to content himself with representing his father at festivities in Hanover. So bad was their relationship that when Frederick predeceased George in 1751, dying from a burst abscess on the lung, the king was heard to comment later the same year, 'I have lost my eldest son, but I was glad of it.'

The king and queen's coronation day ended with the traditional banquet at Westminster Hall, where they sat on chairs of state at the upper end of the vast room. According to the *London Gazette*, that part of the ceremony was performed 'with the greatest Splendour and Magnificence, and without any disaster'.

The royal couple left for St James's Palace before 8 p.m., but the celebrations continued: 'The day concluded with Bonfires, Illuminations, Ringing of Bells and other publick Demonstrations of a general Joy and Satisfaction.'

GEORGE III
1760–1820

Unlike the first two Georges, George III wanted very much to recover the Crown's authority over parliament. His period of personal rule ended when his favoured minister, Lord North, effectively mismanaged rule over the American colonies, which broke away from Britain in 1776 at the end of the War of Independence. George married Charlotte of Mecklenburg-Strelitz and the couple had nine sons and six daughters. The king had a passionate interest in the agricultural developments that took place during his reign and was dubbed 'Farmer George'. He suffered occasional bouts of mental instability, finally necessitating a regency from 1811, during which his eldest son ruled for him, as prince regent.

Coronation of George III, 22 September 1761

George III's coronation is notable for the huge delay in proceedings before and during the ceremony at Westminster, as well as the inevitable catalogue of mishaps that occurred during the under-rehearsed event.

George III ascended to the throne, at the age of 22, on 25 October 1760, following the death of his grandfather George II. As yet unmarried, he fulfilled this dynastic obligation the following year, choosing the German protestant Princess Charlotte of Mecklenburg-Strelitz. The couple only came face to face on their wedding day, 8 September 1761, just in time for her to be crowned with him on 22 September. Both ceremonies were performed by the Archbishop of Canterbury, Thomas Secker.

By royal standards, George and Charlotte were an unpretentious couple and on their coronation day, rather than driving through the capital in a spectacular carriage procession, they opted to be carried from St James's Palace to Westminster Hall in a pair of his-and-hers sedan chairs. As George's biographer John Brooke states, the regal couple looked 'like ordinary citizens going to the theatre'.

As always, the ceremony attracted large crowds, with some paying 10 guineas each for seats in the abbey complex and one house on the route being leased out for 1,000 guineas. The occupants may have been some of the viewers who cheered the popular statesman William Pitt the Elder, who had recently masterminded victory over the French in the Seven Years War. So rapturous was the public response that the mob hung on to Pitt's carriage, including the wheels, hugged his footmen and even kissed his horses. The royal sedan chairs and their occupants received nothing compared with that.

In Westminster Hall the timetable went awry from when the main participants, as usual, congregated ahead of the service. No one could find the Sword of State so the Earl of Huntingdon, Master of the Horse, improvised by borrowing the Lord Mayor's Pearl Sword instead. The king and queen had no chairs to sit on and there was no canopy to carry over them as they walked in procession to the abbey, so they had to improvise. The royal couple walked on a specially constructed wooden walkway, 3ft (0.9m) high, running from New Palace Yard to the West Door of the abbey. Some 2,800 soldiers of duty largely blocked the view and, at times, used the blunt ends of their swords and muskets for crowd control. George and Charlotte finally arrived for their coronation at 1.30 p.m. to be met by the disgruntled clergy, led by the Dean of Westminster, who had been waiting outside for ninety minutes.

It was to be another two hours before George was finally crowned by Archbishop Secker to cheers from the congregation. Charlotte was then crowned with a specially made crown for the occasion, a precedent that each future queen consort would follow from 1831 to Queen Elizabeth's coronation in 1937. The latter found the service a deeply spiritual moment and eyewitnesses at George and Charlotte's ceremony noted the couple's dignity and 'the reverent attention which both paid'. Before his anointing, the king took off his crown, feeling it more appropriate to receive unction as a man rather than a monarch. In another of the day's mishaps, at this point all the peers took George's action as an instruction and removed their coronets too. The poet Thomas Gray wrote a vivacious account of the service to a friend in which he recalled another slip-up when the dean 'would have dropped the crown if it had not been pinned to the cushion' and 'the King was often obliged to call out and set matters right'.

By the time the archbishop came to deliver his sermon, the congregation was so fatigued by all the delays they took this lull in the proceedings to eat food (mainly cold meat and pies) handed round by their servants. Poor Secker's words were drowned out by the audible clattering of knives and forks on plates as well as the tinkling of glasses as the peers swilled down their snacks with wine.

They fared better than the guests at the coronation banquet in Westminster Hall, though, where the heralds responsible for the seating plan mucked things up to such an extent that some peers found themselves without a seat. 'No dinner to eat, shameful expedients to defraud mob,' grumbled the Duchess of Northumberland, 'instead of profusion of geese, etc, not wherewithal to fill one's belly.' A furious George later reprimanded the Earl of Effingham, the Deputy Earl Marshal and the man ultimately responsible for this part of the ceremony. Effingham apologised and swore 'that the next coronation would be conducted with the greatest order imaginable' – a remark that so tickled the king he asked the courtier to repeat it time and again.

GEORGE IV
1820–1830

George IV became prince regent in 1811 as a result of the mental instability of his father, George III. He succeeded to the throne in January 1820. He had secretly married the Roman Catholic Maria Fitzherbert in 1785. This union was not valid under English law because he had not received the prior approval of the king or the Privy Council, as required by the Royal Marriages Act 1772. In 1795 he married Princess Caroline of Brunswick. Their only child Princess Charlotte died giving birth to a stillborn child in 1817, aged 21. A reckless spendthrift, he built the Royal Pavilion at Brighton, redeveloped both Windsor Castle and Buckingham Palace, and acquired many significant works of art.

Coronation of George IV, 19 July 1821

By the time he reached his mid-thirties, George's spiralling debt had continued to climb and his father would only agree

*George IV with the train of his immense robe being carried by
eight sons of peers and the Master of the Robes. The total cost of the
coronation was £238,000, the most expensive ever and more than
twenty times the cost of his father, George III's, in 1761.*

to help him financially if he married his cousin Caroline of
Brunswick, the daughter of the king's elder sister Augusta.

Their first meeting at St James's Palace didn't augur well.
Caroline knelt in deference to her betrothed, who raised her
and embraced her before memorably telling an aide, 'Harris,
I am not well; pray get me a glass of brandy.'

The wedding took place at the Chapel Royal in April 1795.
One guest, Lord Melbourne, thought the groom looked 'like
a man doing a thing in desperation', adding, 'and he was quite
drunk'. He was literally supported by the dukes of Roxburghe
and Bedford, 'looked like death', and spent his wedding night
under the grate in his apartment, where he had fallen in a stupor.

After the birth of their only child, Princess Charlotte, the
following year, the couple began an acrimonious separation.

Many supported Caroline's cause, including the novelist Jane Austen, who wrote, 'Poor woman, I shall support her as long as I can, because she *is* a Woman and because I hate her Husband.' (Austen's opinion never changed, even though it emerged that George was a huge fan, had a collection of her works in each of his residences and more or less instructed her to dedicate *Emma* to him.)

Caroline left Britain in August 1814 and spent the next six years travelling extensively around Europe with her servant Bartolomeo Pergami, who many, including the poet Lord Byron, assumed was her lover. Then, on 29 January 1820, her father-in-law George III died and nominally she became Queen of the United Kingdom. A few days later, the MP Henry Brougham, who was Caroline's chief advisor, wrote, 'she is extremely popular ... the cry at the proclamation was "God save the Queen", much to the annoyance of her husband.' George resumed divorce proceedings, which were never completed, though he was successful in persuading the Cabinet to agree to drop her name from the liturgy of the Church of England, so the nation henceforth only prayed for the king and the rest of the royal family lumped together.

Caroline decided the time was ripe to return to the land of which she was now queen consort. *The Times* noted breathlessly, 'neither at the landing of William the Conqueror, nor at that of the Earl of Richmond, nor of William III' had any arrival in England caused such a sensation. At Dover, crowds gathered on the beach, the clifftops and along the roads to catch a glimpse of her coming ashore on 5 June 1820. The throng shouted, 'God bless Queen Caroline', and they even unhitched the horses from their traces and manually pulled her carriage through the streets. She was similarly mobbed as she crossed Westminster Bridge to enter the capital.

The following month, the Pains and Penalties Bill 1820 was presented in parliament in an effort to strip Caroline of her title and dissolve her marriage. This amounted to a public trial and the outraged public submitted 800 petitions with nearly a million signatures in favour of Caroline. In July it was announced that the coronation had been postponed indefinitely. George was clearly hoping to rid himself of his wife and queen before proceeding to be crowned in peace. In the event, the bill was passed through the House of Lords but was never submitted to the House of Commons as there was very little chance of the Commons passing it. Caroline was therefore acquitted and awarded £50,000 per annum by the government. Such was the delight, not just in London but throughout the nation, that the leading cities were all illuminated for five nights.

So, George was stuck with his queen consort and had no alternative but to forge ahead with plans for his coronation. There was, however, one tiny glimmer of hope for him on 5 May 1821, when news broke of the death of Napoleon Bonaparte on St Helena. Sir Edward Nagle, Groom of the Bedchamber, rushed to tell the king, 'Sir, your bitterest enemy is dead', to which the hopeful king retorted, 'Is she by God!'

George settled down to prepare the lavish ceremony for which parliament had voted the massive sum of £243,000. Visitors to his Carlton House residence were taken to see his robes on which £24,000 had been spent, with the ermine alone costing £855. Completing the ensemble was a crimson velvet train over 26ft (8m) in length and a huge, black, Spanish hat decorated with ostrich feathers and heron plumes.

Preparations were also being undertaken by the queen, who had applied to the Home Secretary for a formal application to be crowned as consort. The matter was raised in the Commons, where the members rather chickened out by deciding it was

George's prerogative whether or not Caroline should take part in the service. Still hedging her bets, the queen had fittings for her and her two ladies for suitable gowns for the big day.

Caroline made it clear she intended to be present, even though the prime minister, Lord Liverpool, tried to dissuade her. On the day itself she arrived at the door to the East Cloister of Westminster Abbey, which she found barred to her, as was the one leading to the West Cloister. She then crossed to Westminster Hall, where the king would lead the procession from. Here she shouted, 'Let me past; I am your queen!' but the soldiers on duty blocked her path and held their bayonets under her chin, and the Deputy Lord Chamberlain had the door slammed shut in her face. In one desperate attempt at admission, Caroline crossed back to the abbey and tried to gain access via the door at Poet's Corner (the one used by Elizabeth II at the memorial service for the Duke of Edinburgh in March 2022). Here, Sir Robert Inglis persuaded her to give up her attempts, advising her to go away. The fickle London crowds, not so long ago rioting in her favour, now booed her and ridiculed the very undignified spectacle of her resorting to begging for admission.

With Caroline safely on her way back to Cambridge House, George arrived at Westminster Hall at 10.30 a.m., half an hour late. The artist Benjamin Haydon witnessed the king's impressive arrival: 'Something rustles, and a being buried in satin, feathers and diamonds rolls gracefully into his seat.' The plump and rather dissolute figure holding centre stage with his brown wig of curls cascading over his forehead could have looked comical. According to the following day's *Times*, many were, however, surprised at the dignity with which George behaved. 'The young people in particular', who had gone 'merely with the expectation of a show', were 'taken by surprise and found themselves affected in a manner they never dreamt of'.

George walked along a carpet strewn with herbs – a centuries-old tradition to ward off plague – with the regalia borne before him. Eager to be seen, he instructed the Cinque Port knights not to hide him with the canopy but to carry it nearby. He was also keen for his pages to display his crimson velvet train to full effect and was heard to twice call out, 'Hold it wider.'

Inside the abbey, crammed with guests, it was so hot the king appeared distressed and almost fainted. One guest, Lady Cowper, thought 'several times he was at the last gasp', though he managed to fortify himself with doses of sal volatile. The ceremony lasted five hours and, as the king withdrew to change into his final processional robes, the peers, peeresses, ambassadors, musicians, singers and nearly everyone else rushed outside for a breath of fresh air. When the newly crowned king reappeared, he was therefore faced with the sight of 'empty benches covered with dirt and litter and the backs of his courtiers expediting their exits'.

Shortly after four o'clock, George entered Westminster Hall for what would be the last coronation banquet ever staged in this country, with 300 guests waiting to dine with the king, on turtle soup, a dish of quails and slices of capon. A highlight was the last entry on horseback of the King's Champion, this time in the person of Sir Henry Dymoke, who was accompanied by the Duke of Wellington.

The king departed for Carlton House at half past seven, leaving the peers to consume the mountains of food remaining. The festivities continued with gun salutes, church bells ringing and fireworks in Hyde Park. George was no doubt pleased to have received, in the words of the novelist Sir Walter Scott, a 'general welcome from his subjects'. Meanwhile, Caroline moved on to Brandenburg House, where she entertained friends to supper and was observed trying to be genial but 'while she laughed tears rolled down her face – tears of anguish'.

The following day Sir Walter Scott, continuing his account of coronation day, declared Caroline was 'a fire of straw which has now burnt to the very embers, and those who try to blow it into light again will only blacken their hands and noses, like mischievous children dabbling among the ashes of the bonfire'. Anyone hoping to ignite the royal embers wouldn't have had long to try since the night after the coronation she fell ill, possibly with cancer, and her health deteriorated over the next three weeks. When it became clear she was dying, she put her affairs in order, including her funeral arrangements. She was to be buried in her native Brunswick in a tomb, which she asked should bear the inscription: 'Here lies Caroline, the Injured Queen of England.'

George's reputation never really recovered from his profligacy and unseemly marriage difficulties. He spent his final years at Windsor in befuddled seclusion, often telling guests that he had been present at the Battle of Waterloo, which was untrue. Following his funeral in June 1830, *The Times* offered the excoriating editorial: 'There never was an individual less regretted by his fellow-creatures than this deceased King.'

WILLIAM IV
1830–1837

Until the accession of Charles III, William IV had held the record as the oldest person to succeed to the British throne. He was 64 years old when he became king following the death of his brother George IV in June 1830. He had served in the Royal Navy from the age of 13, being present at the Battle of Cape St Vincent in 1780 and later serving under Horatio Nelson. In 1818 he married Princess Adelaide of Saxe-Meiningen. His seven-year reign witnessed the Reform Act of 1832, aimed at improving the electoral system, and the abolition of slavery in most of the British Empire.

Coronation of William IV, 8 September 1831

William IV was no fan of pageantry. Despite being chief mourner at his brother's funeral, he talked loudly and incessantly throughout the service at St George's Chapel, Windsor. After enduring two hours of obsequies, he stood up while the anthem was played, shook hands with the Earl Marshal and walked out. The Tory MP Lord Ellenborough commented, 'a coronation could hardly be gayer.'

At his first Privy Council as monarch, William foreshadowed Charles III's annoyance with a pen holder cluttering the table at his own accession council, by shouting out, 'This is a damned bad pen you have given me!'

It was therefore no surprise that he told his prime minister, Lord Grey, that he regarded a coronation as a 'useless and ill-timed expense' and that he wanted to avoid such a public spectacle. In fact, just as Meghan Markle apparently believed she was married by the Archbishop of Canterbury three days before the actual ceremony, so William IV believed his coronation took place in private months before the actual service; the reason being that William had been asked by Grey to dissolve parliament after the First Reform Bill was defeated in the House of Commons. The new king agreed to attend parliament in person. He also insisted the crown should be brought to Westminster, although he had no right to wear it ahead of the coronation. Entering the Robing Room, prior to processing to the House of Lords, William picked up the crown, placed it on his head and announced to Grey: 'Now, my lord, the Coronation is over!'

William, again like Charles III, was concerned about holding an extravagant ceremony of state when the public was experiencing dire economic need, particularly as it was only ten years since his brother's embarrassingly profligate coronation. The king made it clear he would prefer simply making an oath before both houses of parliament. Grey persuaded him to rethink, and William reluctantly agreed, providing it could be, in his words, 'short and cheap'. Various Tory ministers announced they would boycott such a workaday crowning, to which William responded, 'I anticipate from that greater convenience of room and less heat.'

William's reform of the ceremony was radical. Dropping both the elaborate procession from Westminster Hall and the traditional post-coronation banquet, also held in the hall, saved thousands of pounds. Although they wouldn't see him in a stately procession on foot, the public would instead have the bonus of witnessing a carriage procession, the highlight of which was William and his consort, Queen Adelaide, in the Gold State Coach. They also had greater access to the new monarch's court, based at St James's Palace, thanks to William opening the 'New Avenue', which later became the Mall and which was illuminated for the festivities.

He vetoed a full-dress affair, so the attendant peers wore their parliamentary rather than ceremonial robes. The Earl Marshal's pages each wore a blue frock coat and white breeches teamed with a crimson sash and a plumed hat, all paid for by their parents. The king himself donned no vestments other than a royal robe and he refused the traditional girding with a sword and the presentation of gold armils. He would have liked to have banned another tradition as well: having to kiss his bishops – a practice the Archbishop of Canterbury, William Howley, insisted should remain.

The pared-down ceremony saw the ending of the tradition that barons from the Cinque Port coastal towns of Kent and Sussex should carry the canopy over the monarch during the coronation. Afterwards pieces of the cloth were sold, with the proceeds going to the relevant towns. The tradition dated back at least to Richard I's coronation, when it was documented that four barons carried a silk canopy balanced on four spears above the king as he processed into the abbey.

William also saved money by using old state chairs from St James's Palace and the House of Lords for principal guests to sit on. His Coronation Chair, together with Queen Adelaide's, can still be seen at Chatsworth House in Derbyshire, where they were taken as a perquisite by the 6th Duke of Devonshire, who was the king's Lord Chamberlain.

Shopping around also helped the royal coffers. When Rundells, the court goldsmiths, offered to make seven coronets for the royal dukes and duchesses for £50 all in, they were undercut by the company of Green and Ward, which offered to do them for £10 less. Queen Adelaide decided not to follow recent tradition and hire gemstones for her crown, telling Charles Greville, Clerk of the Privy Council, 'I have got jewels enough, so I will have them made up myself', offering to pay for it too. Of the £15,000 put aside for the coronation jewellery, only £1,453 19s 8d was spent.

Variously labelled the 'Penny Coronation' and the 'Half Crown-ation', the coronation of William IV was a welcome contrast to that of George IV and, at £43,159, was less than a fifth of the older brother's £238,000 extravaganza. It was a public relations coup and endeared him to his people, who were unused to a monarch who was good humoured, accessible and clearly didn't waste public funds (or his own). Countess Lieven, wife of the Russian ambassador, wrote breathlessly about the upsurge in affection his subjects had for the new king: 'From grave and depressed they have become possessed of a gaiety, a vivacity, and a movement that makes them scarcely recognizable.' As Charles Greville noted about William's coronation in his infamous memoirs, 'whereas nobody was satisfied before it, everybody was after it'.

VICTORIA
1837–1901

Victoria was the longest-reigning British monarch until, in September 2015, Elizabeth II broke this record. She succeeded to the throne, aged 18, in June 1837 and was still unmarried at the time of her coronation. Victoria and her morally upright husband, Prince Albert of Saxe-Coburg-Gotha, gave the monarchy respectability. The birth of nine children and a happy domestic life that would be shared with the public through the medium of photography brought Crown and people closer than ever. Her reign saw great technical inventions, from the development of the railway system through to the motor car, as well as the invention of the telephone and of 'moving pictures'. Controversially today, her reign also saw the British Empire double in size with the acquisition of huge swathes of Africa and in 1876 Victoria became Empress of India.

Coronation of Victoria, 28 June 1838

We usually have to rely on chroniclers or eyewitnesses for detail of British coronations, but Queen Victoria, whose journals stretched over a seventy-year period from 1831 to her death in

Victoria looking serene as she receives the sacrament during her coronation. It was a ceremony packed with disasters, from the archbishop forcing the coronation ring on to the wrong finger to him then trying to give her the orb she had already received.
(Library of Congress)

1901, left a detailed account of over 2,300 words recording her red-letter day. Two things stand out from her account. Firstly, it was a public spectacle with the journey to and from the abbey taking an hour each way, along an extended route that would become the template for twentieth-century coronations. Secondly, since there were almost no rehearsals, certainly by the queen and the senior clergy, there was a whole catalogue of disasters, from the coronation ring being jammed on to the wrong royal finger to the trainbearers making a hash of carrying the queen's robes.

Victoria was the first monarch to take up official residence in Buckingham Palace after it was transformed into an imposing three-sided mansion by John Nash in the 1820s. One of the problems for the monarch of the day has always been the palace's very public location next to the royal parks, accessible, at least at the front, to generations of gawping crowds, as the Queen recorded in her journal on coronation day: 'I was awoke at four o'clock by the guns in the Park, and could not get much sleep afterwards on account of the noise of the people, bands, &c.,&c.'

Her lack of sleep didn't seem to affect her mood and there were no signs of pre-coronation jitters: 'Got up at 7 feeling strong and well; the Park presented a curious spectacle; crowds of people up to Constitution Hill, soldiers, bands, &c. I dressed, having taken a little breakfast before I dressed, and a little after.'

London was abuzz with excitement, with 400,000 visitors crammed into the capital, many arriving on one of the new-fangled trains from the suburbs. Hyde Park had become a vast encampment for those trying to snatch a few hours' sleep before heading to secure a place along the processional route.

The diarist George Greville enthused, 'There was never anything seen like the state of this town, it is as if the population had been on a sudden quadrupled; the uproar, the confusion, the crowds, the noise, are indescribable.'

The government budgeted £70,000 for the event – a compromise between the £240,000 lavished on George IV's overblown celebration and the modest £30,000 'Half Crownation' of his younger brother William IV.

Some of the expense went on stands for the public, with galleries and scaffolding lining much of the route. There was much for the crowds to see. Victoria left the palace at ten o'clock in the Gold State Coach drawn by cream horses brought across from Hanover. The coach, with its panelled artwork by Giovanni Cipriani, glittered in the glorious morning sun. Inside was the slender figure of the 19-year-old queen, wearing her crimson velvet parliament robes over an embroidered white satin dress and a diamond circlet. From Buckingham Palace, the 4-tonne coach lumbered at a walking pace towards Hyde Park Corner, along Piccadilly, towards Whitehall. Despite its beauty, the coach has always offered a terrible ride for its royal occupant. Her predecessor, William IV (the 'Sailor King'), said it was like a 'ship tossing in a rough sea' – and he would have known. Despite the roads of London being slowly upgraded using water-bound macadam, Victoria still felt the Gold State Coach's 'distressing oscillations'.

The queen was overwhelmed by the sheer scale of the welcome en route to the abbey:

It was a fine day; and the crowds of people exceeded what I have ever seen … the millions of my loyal subjects who were assembled in every spot to witness the Procession. Their good-humour and excessive loyalty was beyond everything, and I really cannot say how proud I feel to be the Queen of such a Nation.

She was even alarmed 'at times for fear that the people would be crushed and squeezed on account of the tremendous rush and pressure'.

Victoria had been nervous in the days ahead of the ceremony. Prime Minister Viscount Melbourne, her beloved 'Lord M', offered her the hackneyed reassurance: 'Oh you'll like it when you're there.'

It turned out he was right. As she arrived at the abbey shortly after 11.30 a.m., one eyewitness inside thought her as 'gay as a lark … like a girl on her birthday'. Arthur Stanley, later Dean of Windsor, seated in one of the specially constructed galleries, felt the rails quiver as everyone lunged forward to get a better view of the queen.

From then on things went downhill. According to the historian Sir Roy Strong, 'the ceremony of 1838 was the last of the botched coronations'. The queen doesn't appear to have rehearsed at all and only visited the abbey the evening before at the insistence of Melbourne: 'I'm very glad I went to the Abbey as I shall now know exactly where I am to go, and be.' In fact, on the day she didn't have much of a clue. According to Lord St John, the sub-dean, there was 'a continual difficulty and embarrassment, and the Queen never knew what she was to do'.

Things got off to a bad start when her maids of honour, in virginal white like their monarch, carried Victoria's ermine-trimmed robe but kept falling over their own trains. One of them recalled that 'we carried the Queen's train very jerkily and badly, never keeping step as she did', much to the annoyance of the Duchess of Sutherland, Mistress of the Robes, and in effect their boss on the day.

After making the oath to govern 'the Protestant reformed religion as it is established by law', followed by her anointing, the queen retired to St Edward's Chapel, which she thought was 'a dark small place'. She was unimpressed that 'what was called an Altar was covered with sandwiches, bottles of wine, etc, etc.' Here she changed into 'a singular gown of linen trimmed with lace' and a supertunica made from cloth of gold embellished with the floral symbols of the United Kingdom, before processing to St Edward's Chair to be crowned.

St Edward's Crown was far too heavy for the tiny Victoria to cope with so the Crown Jewellers, Rundell, Bridge & Co., made the Imperial State Crown using a total of 3,093 gems. Victoria noted in her journal, 'the Crown being placed on my head ... was, I must own, a most beautiful impressive moment'. She was less impressed when the Archbishop of Canterbury jammed the coronation ring, made to fit her little finger, on to her ring finger 'and the consequence was that I had the greatest difficulty to take it off again – which I at last did with great pain'. The archbishop also tried to give her the orb, which she had already received from him. 'He (as usual),' she wrote, 'was so confused and puzzled and knew nothing and went away.' The Bishop of Durham, who was standing next to her, completely lost his place in the order of service while the Bishop of Bath and Wells turned over two pages by mistake, sent Victoria off to St Edward's Chapel far too early and had to go and bring her back to fill in the section he'd omitted. 'Pray tell me what I am to do,' Victoria asked the sub-dean, Lord Thynne, 'for they don't know.'

At least the dodgy ritual gave the congregation something to reflect on. The future prime minister Benjamin Disraeli lamented 'the want of rehearsal', felt Lord M held the Sword of State 'like a butcher' and spotted Lord Ward, with his coronet askew, knocking back champagne from a pewter pot.

Also scathing was the social theorist Harriet Martineau (whose fourth great-grandniece is Catherine, Princess of Wales), who was personally invited by Victoria as she admired her writing. Even though she had a free seat at the most prestigious event of the year, Martineau thought the whole thing 'highly barbaric' and 'worthy only of the old Pharaonic times in Egypt'. She felt the whole ritual was 'offensive ... to the God of the nineteenth century in the Western world'. Once started there was clearly no stopping her vitriol; the peeresses, she thought, were:

> Old hags, with their dyed or false hair drawn to the top of the head, to allow the putting on of the coronet, had their necks and arms bare and glittering with diamonds: and those necks and arms were so brown and wrinkled as to make one sick.

There was, however, concern for the aptly named Lord Rolle, aged 82, who, according to Victoria, was:

> dreadfully infirm [and], in attempting to ascend the steps, fell and rolled quite down, but was not the least hurt; when he attempted to re-ascend them, I got up and advanced to the end of the steps, in order to prevent another fall.

This was greeted with shouts of approval from the congregation. The queen also noted 'when Lord Melbourne's turn to do Homage came, there was loud cheering; they also cheered Lord Grey and the Duke of Wellington'.

After five hours in the abbey and two changes of dress, the queen was ready to leave:

> At about ½ p.4 I re-entered my carriage, the Crown on my head, and Sceptre and Orb in my hand, and we proceeded the same way as we came – the crowds if possible

having increased. The enthusiasm, affection and loyalty was really touching, and I shall ever remember this day as the proudest of my life.

HOUSE OF
SAXE-COBURG-GOTHA
AND HOUSE OF WINDSOR
<u>1901–PRESENT DAY</u>

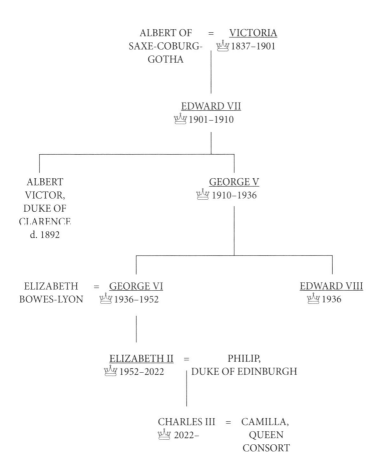

EDWARD VII
1901–1910

Albert Edward, Prince of Wales, became king at the age of 59. He had been given no training by Queen Victoria, who refused to allow him access to government papers. His short reign of nine years showed a marked increase in the ceremonial role of the monarch thanks to Edward's love of pageantry, in sharp contrast to his mother's reluctance to appear in public during her four-decade widowhood. Known as Edward the Peacemaker, the king was a natural diplomat. The Entente Cordiale with France was boosted by his personal involvement and ended Britain's isolation in Europe. He was a notable racehorse owner, winning the 1909 Derby with his horse Minoru.

Coronation of Edward VII, 9 August 1902

An emergency operation wrecked the original plans for the coronation of Edward VII. On 23 June 1902, three days before the service was due to take place, the king, with Queen Alexandra, returned to London in preparation for the festivities. On the return journey, he developed a high fever and excruciating pain.

His doctors diagnosed an abdominal abscess, which could cause death by blood poisoning without surgery. Initially, the king refused to consider it, telling Francis Laking, his physician-in-ordinary, 'The Coronation cannot be postponed. I won't hear of it. I cannot and will not disappoint the people. I will go the Abbey on Thursday if I die there.' Laking's reply was straightforward: 'If Your Majesty did go on Thursday to the Abbey, in all human probability you would die there.'

The following morning, forty-eight hours before the coronation was scheduled to take place, a statement was issued from Buckingham Palace announcing its postponement and the king's need for surgery. This was conducted on an operating table in what was usually Edward's dressing room.

A major concern for his physicians was the 60-year-old patient's ability to withstand a general anaesthetic, not to mention the surgery itself. Known to his friends, mostly behind his back, as 'Tum Tum', the king was known to eat five-course breakfasts, followed by luncheon, afternoon tea and a twelve-course dinner at 9 p.m. By the time of his coronation, his waist measured the same as his chest, 48in (122cm). Queen Alexandra said her husband's appetite was 'appalling' and that she had 'never seen anything like it'. Moreover, he smoked eleven to thirteen cigars, mostly giant Havanas, each day, as well as more than twenty Egyptian cigarettes.

Queen Alexandra was determined to stay with her husband throughout the procedure, until the specialist, Sir Fredrick Treves, embarrassed at the thought of rolling his sleeves up in front of the royal consort, asked her to leave. Although many, including Edward's grandson the Duke of Windsor in his memoirs, believed the king had had his appendix removed, in fact the cause of the agony was perityphlitis, an inflammation around the appendix. This appeared as a large abscess, which Treves cut and then drained with tubes.

Meanwhile, outside the palace, members of the public gathered for the latest bulletins. Rumours of cancer were circulating and at the Carlton Hotel, one of the king's favourite haunts, the proprietor César Ritz suffered a nervous collapse, more to do with having to cancel his coronation dinner for 500 guests than the loss of his most distinguished patron.

Edward's recovery appears to have been swift. His grandson the Duke of Windsor recalled, 'My father liked to tell how he found King Edward next day sitting up in bed at Buckingham Palace enjoying a long cigar.' Before the day was out, he'd invited his mistress, Alice Keppel (great-grandmother of Queen Camilla), round for tea and begun reading *The Hound of the Baskervilles.*

Preparations for the delayed coronation were largely in the hands of Reginald Brett, 2nd Viscount Esher, who had elevated Queen Victoria's 1897 Diamond Jubilee into a vast imperial pageant. Nearly all the heads of state and VIPs congregated in London for the scheduled ceremony had returned home. The king's niece Princess Marie Louise remembered, 'the Coronation itself was a much more intimate, I might also say family, celebration.' Esher was able to replicate the mood of the jubilee with its focus on this family of nations over which Edward ruled. The composer Edward Elgar reflected the jingoistic fervour by marrying his 'Pomp and Circumstance March No.1' with the word of Eton housemaster A.C. Benson's 'Coronation Ode' to create 'Land of Hope and Glory'.

Edward and Alexandra were finally crowned on 9 August 1902, before a congregation of 8,000 in the abbey (four times the amount of seating for Prince William's wedding to Catherine Middleton in 2011).

Given the king's recent illness, various changes were made to the original order of service. The sermon was omitted and the litany was chanted in the procession before Edward's arrival. The king agreed that, instead of being crowned with the magnificent solid gold St Edward's Crown, weighing 4.9lb (2.23kg), he would use the lighter Imperial State Crown. Even with these modifications, it was stressful for the royal family to watch the recently ill monarch partake in the lengthy service. His niece Princess Alice, Countess of Athlone, recalled in the 1960s, 'we all watched him with some anxiety.'

Other eyewitnesses recalled the touching moment when the king's heir, George, Prince of Wales, knelt to pay homage to his sovereign and Edward pulled him back by his robes and kissed him twice.

The delay of forty-four days in crowning the king allowed for more rehearsal time, although there were still the inevitable glitches in the ceremony. When Alexandra arrived at the Great West Door, the choir of Westminster schoolboys proclaimed her '*Vivat Regina Alexandra*' out of time with the anthem. The same boys similarly mucked up '*Vivat Rex Edwardus*', coming in too early and needing to shout it again to fit in with Hubert Parry's 'I was Glad When They Said Unto Me'.

Eighty-year-old William Temple, the officiating Archbishop of Canterbury, proved a liability. He put the Imperial State Crown the wrong way round on the king's head, which Edward deftly corrected. He was nearly blind and had to have the order of service printed in enormous text on scrolls held by his bishops. Finally, he was so frail that when he knelt to pay homage to his sovereign he couldn't rise again and the king and the bishops helped hoist him to his feet, although the ungrateful prelate snapped 'go away!' to one holy aide, which was clearly heard throughout the quire.

Another unexpected noise came from the king's youngest sister Princess Beatrice, seated in the royal box immediately above a lavish display of silver gilt altar dishes. According to her niece Princess Marie Louise, Beatrice 'was very proud of her bound and specially-embroidered copy of the Coronation service'. Unfortunately, she was also prone to fidgeting and realised to her horror, '"Louie it's going – oh dear, it's gone!" And gone it had with a terrible clatter among the church plate.'

Meanwhile, Queen Alexandra had her own dilemma. She had asked to be anointed by the archbishop on her forehead rather than her head, mainly because she wore a wig and felt that she wouldn't benefit from the sacred moment if the holy oil didn't touch her body. A sign of the cross was duly made on her brow, but the residue started to trickle down her nose and, fearing it would be irreverent to wipe it off with her handkerchief, she opted to regally drip.

In later life Princess Alice recalled the king and queen receiving 'a terrific ovation … everybody was very excited by the novelty of the occasion, as it was the first Coronation to take place in England for over sixty years'. The feeling of respect and affection was mutual, and, like Elizabeth II on her twenty-first birthday, he vowed to dedicate his life to their service. He wrote a personal address 'To My People', telling them: 'I now offer up my deepest gratitude to Divine Providence for having preserved my life and given me strength to fulfil the important duties which devolve on me as Sovereign.'

GEORGE V
1910–1936

Like his son George VI, George V was a second son, born with little expectation of becoming king. In his case, it was the death of his older brother Prince Albert Victor, Duke of Clarence, from pneumonia, in January 1892, which forced George to give up a promising naval career to take up full-time royal duties. His reign of twenty-five years saw the monarchy grow closer to all classes of subjects for several reasons. Firstly, during the First World War the king travelled to France and Belgium, visiting hospitals and reviewing troops. Secondly, the demise of the Russian, German and Austro-Hungarian monarchies at the end of the conflict, George and his consort made a concerted effort to cross the class divide and visit industrial heartlands. Finally, his introduction of the royal Christmas broadcast from 1932 was an initiative that increased the bond between king and people.

Coronation of George V, 22 June 1911

The second coronation of the twentieth century had several 'firsts'. It was the first to be photographed from inside the abbey; it was the first to use the newly developed processional route through the Mall and Whitehall; it was the first of three to be followed within days by a thanksgiving service at St Paul's Cathedral; and it was the first to feature the iconic balcony appearance following the return journey to Buckingham Palace.

Edward VII embraced pageantry and splendour as much as his mother disliked both of them. It was very much his wish to transform the roadways from Buckingham Palace to Westminster into boulevards that rivalled the city-centre architecture of Paris, Rome and Vienna. The architect Aston Webb, responsible for the façade of the Victoria and Albert Museum, was given the commission. Work had begun on extending and widening the Mall and constructing Admiralty Arch by the time of Edward's death in May 1910. In the run-up to the coronation, insurance buildings near the entrance to Whitehall were demolished, creating an 88ft-wide (26.8m) opening to the Mall. *The Times* felt 'this is perhaps the most striking of the changes that are being wrought in the aspect of London in connexion with the Coronation', adding it 'offered a fine view to the traveller westwards along the Strand'.

Blocking the view were some of the fifty stands erected along the route accommodating between 250 and 3,500 people in their wooden structures. A total of 2,134 tonnes of timber was used, held in place by a further 71 tonnes of nuts, bolts and screws.

George V and his consort Queen Mary of Teck photographed in all their regal splendour following the coronation. They would later make history by being the first king and queen to appear on the balcony of Buckingham Palace while wearing their crowns and robes.
(Pictorial Press Ltd/Alamy Stock Photo)

Suitably majestic buildings such as the Old War Office, opened in 1906, and Central Hall, opposite Westminster Abbey, completed five years later, lined the ceremonial way. In 1911 they were a perfect backdrop for the parade of 45,000 imperial troops representing the dominions of Canada,

Australia, New Zealand and South Africa, as well as India, West and East Africa, Ceylon, Malaya and the West Indies.

In the abbey, another procession included Prime Minister Herbert Asquith; the Archbishop of Canterbury, Randall Davidson; Frank Dymoke, the King's Champion, carrying the flag of England; the Duke of Wellington, bearing the union flag; Lord Roberts, carrying the sword of spiritual justice; and Lord Kitchener, carrying the sword of temporal justice.

A congregation of 7,139 was present in the abbey to witness the coronation. The peerage count was whittled down slightly by not inviting the peers' daughters, widows and eldest sons, but the massed ranks in the seats and stands were still overwhelmingly blue-blooded. This benefitted the ushers on duty, one of whom later picked up three ropes of pearls, three-quarters of a diamond necklace, twenty brooches, six or seven bracelets and twenty gold balls knocked off coronets. It was estimated that his haul of abandoned jewels came to £20,000. Presumably it wasn't the done thing to have a lost property office in the abbey environs.

The coronation committee meeting of 31 October 1910 had mooted the idea of working-class representation. In the event, the members decided on the token gesture of just two seats each to the Trades Congress Parliamentary Committee, the National Confederation of Friendly Societies and the Central Board of the Co-operative Union.

Three working people who did have places were the official photographer and two artists. Benjamin Stone was a photographer trusted by the king to photograph intimate portraits, such as Edward VII's coffin in the royal vault. He clearly wasn't trusted by the Archbishop of Canterbury, though, who made sure Stone and his camera were 'in a position absolutely concealed'. This presumably accounts for why his view of the king seated on the Coronation Chair is almost blocked.

John Henry Frederick Bacon was commissioned to paint the official picture of the coronation and may have used some artistic licence to produce a clear view of the king in profile and Queen Mary directly facing the viewer. Bacon was hidden from view behind the tombs of Aymer de Valence and Aveline of Lancaster, directly facing the Royal Box.

King George's account of the day in his journal is typical of the man. There is no grand or sweeping statement about the importance of the day; instead, he opens with that most British of subjects – the weather: 'It was overcast & cloudy with some showers & a strongish cool breeze, but better for the people than great heat.' This was, after all, the countryman who tapped his barometer on the wall of York Cottage, on the Sandringham estate, to see what the gods had in store ahead of a day's shooting.

His concern and admiration for 'the people' is again a recurrent theme in the king's journal entries. On this coronation day, he writes, 'There were hundreds of thousands of people who gave us a magnificent reception.' A quarter of century later, after his Silver Jubilee service, the frail king told his nurse, 'I'd no idea they felt that about me … I am beginning to think they must really like me for myself.'

Both George and his consort, Queen Mary, personified the stiff-upper-lip attitude of their generation. Outwardly formidably regal, inwardly they were both traumatised by the coronation. 'The service in the Abbey was most beautiful, but it was a terrible ordeal,' noted George in his journal. 'It was an awful ordeal for us both,' echoed the queen in a letter to her aunt, Augusta of Mecklenburg-Strelitz. *The Times* reported that the king 'wore a very serious expression and looked somewhat tired'. Similarly, the Master of Elibank, an eyewitness in the abbey, thought Mary 'was almost shrinking as she went up the aisle'. On her return journey, perhaps buoyed by her anointing and crowning as well as witnessing the king's, Elibank noted a distinct change: 'she was magnetic, as if she had undergone some marvellous transformation.'

One very personal moment recalled the previous coronation. 'I nearly broke down,' wrote the king, 'when dear David came to do homage to me, as it reminded me so much when I did the same thing to beloved Papa.' David was the Prince of Wales, the heir who, two decades later, would cause his own papa such grief because of his infatuation with the divorced American socialite Wallis Simpson. But on this occasion, the prince knelt and paid homage to his father, touched the crown and kissed him on the right cheek. Clearly moved, King George pulled his son back and kissed him on his left cheek. Edward VII had embraced George in a similar moving gesture.

One significant change from the format of the previous coronation was in the wording of the oath. Edward VII thought it far too anti-Catholic and was in danger of alienating his Roman Catholic subjects. He made it clear that his heir should not 'have to make such a declaration in such a crude way'. The traditional oath was amended, and George V said, 'I ... declare that I am a faithful Protestant and that I will ... secure the Protestant succession to the Throne of my Realm.' George VI and Elizabeth II would repeat the same vow.

Following the service, the king and queen returned to Buckingham Palace in the Gold State Coach via an extended route along Pall Mall, St James Street, Piccadilly and Constitution Hill. At one point, onlookers witnessed a punch-up in the carriage carrying the royal children when the 11-year-old Prince Henry and his 8-year-old brother Prince George laid into each other. Their older sister Princess Mary tried to separate them and nearly had her coronet knocked flying by the fractious pair.

Back at the palace, the king and queen made the first corona-tion day appearance of a monarch on the Buckingham Palace balcony, though it had been used for other royal appearances dating back to the Crimean War. It was still such a rare occur-rence that soldiers on duty broke ranks, put their helmets on the end of their rifles and joined in the cheering.

EDWARD VIII
20 JANUARY 1936–
11 DECEMBER 1936

Edward VIII, known to his family as 'David', reigned for more or less a complete calendar year, so as sovereign he attended nearly every major annual event, from Trooping the Colour to the State Opening of Parliament. As a bachelor king, he performed all of these functions without the presence of a consort by his side. What the public didn't know, thanks to an establishment cover up including the press barons, the prime minister, the Archbishop of Canterbury and nearly all high society, was that the king had, for several years, been besotted by a divorced American socialite called Wallis Simpson. While the British public was kept bliss-fully ignorant of the romance, it was a hot topic in the European press, where paparazzi photos of the couple swimming during a Mediterranean cruise were splashed across many newspapers. The story only broke in the UK when, on 1 December 1936, the Bishop of Bradford made a speech criticising Edward's notable indifference to churchgoing, particularly in light of the forth-coming coronation. The story was picked up by the following day's newspapers; gradually they added to it details of the king's romance and it snowballed into a major constitutional crisis, resulting in Edward abdicating only eight days later.

The country was divided between those who were outraged that the head of the Church of England was prepared to consider marriage to a divorcée, and those less censorious who were saddened that the country could lose the hugely charismatic and popular Edward. It would be at least another half-century before details of Edward's pro-Nazi feelings and his cavalier attitude to what he termed 'royalling' became fully known. Important documents were sometimes returned in the government red boxes with cocktail stains on them and he once memorably cancelled an engagement at Aberdeen Hospital at the last moment, only to be seen meeting Wallis at a railway station. Even without the Mrs Simpson, crisis, he would, in all probability, have been a disastrous monarch.

Never Crowned

Edward VIII was due to be crowned on 12 May 1937, the date that his brother George VI chose for his ceremony, since preparations for the event were already well under way by the time of Edward's abdication.

Curiously, in his 1951 memoirs, *A King's Story*, Edward, by then Duke of Windsor, makes no reference to his involvement in preparations for the coronation. His brother George VI had not allowed either the duke or his ghostwriter access to the royal archives for the book, so this may, in part, account for the omission. In his authorised official biography of Edward VIII, historian Philip Ziegler discovered the king showed little interest in the minutiae of planning the event and deputised much of the work to his brother, and eventual successor, Albert, Duke of York, perhaps even then realising that it would be

Edward V and Edward VIII were the only two monarchs not to have been crowned since the Norman Conquest. The latter was not therefore entitled to wear either the robe of estate or the crown at the 1936 State Opening of Parliament, opting instead for the uniform of an Admiral of the Fleet.

'Bertie' rather than himself who would be crowned by the archbishop the following May.

George V had died on 20 January 1936 and, although full court mourning would last for six months, followed by half-mourning for a further three months, it was necessary to press on with preparations for the coronation.*

The most important thing was to know the actual date, since representatives from the empire as well as overseas regiments connected to the Crown would need to plan their arrival. In Britain the coronation would need everything: seating in the abbey and along the routes, official souvenirs to be designed and made, for peers and peeresses to hire coronets and robes or repair the ones they had stowed away in their mansions.

Preparations had already begun. On 13 March it was reported that 1,000 Australian ex-servicemen and -women who had served in the Great War were planning to attend. All they had to go on at that stage was that it was likely to be next year. In Canada they thought this was a certainty, since on 25 March it was revealed that 'number plates of motor-cars in Ontario are to be coloured "Coronation red" next year'. That same month Westminster Abbey announced it was propos-ing to raise £20,000 for a new organ, using the same pipes, and that an anonymous donor had given £5,000. Newspapers linked this with the coronation, but plans had already been afoot for a few years.

On 2 April 1936, the prime minister Stanley Baldwin told the House of Commons: 'I am in a position to announce, with the approval of His Majesty, that the Coronation will take place

---

* Court mourning for Queen Victoria was an entire year. Elizabeth II announced in 1952 that mourning for her father George VI would be for just over sixteen weeks, while seventy years later her own period of mourning was for just two weeks.

sometime in the month of May next year. The precise date will be announced as soon as possible.' That was about as much as he was going to reveal. Pressed by a Captain MacDonald if troops from the overseas dominions and colonies as well as India would be invited, Baldwin replied, 'I suppose so.'

As *The Times* pointed out, in fixing the date, 'care will be taken to see that the arrangements do not clash with the Whitsuntide Holidays when railway traffic is always very high'.

Tentative plans began straight away. An advert in the same newspaper on the 7th said, 'sites for erections of stands or suitable premises for viewing are wanted.' By 22 May, it was reported that Birmingham firms were already preparing for the big day, with one having to build a new workshop to cope with the demand for flag manufacture. Flags turned out to be a sore point when it was discovered that a consignment of 250 cases of silk flags was being produced in Japan to be shipped over for the event. On 22 June, the Silk Association of Great Britain and Ireland wrote to the President of the Board of Trade urging that all flags and decorations relating to the coronation should be British made.

A Privy Council meeting held on 28 May fixed the date for the coronation as Wednesday 12 May, four days ahead of Whitsunday. The announcement was made in four proclamation ceremonies at 10 a.m. on the day after the meeting. These were held at Friary Court in St James's Palace, Temple Bar, Charing Cross and the Royal Exchange, and it was broadcast live by the BBC in a thirty-minute radio programme.

On 3 July, a special committee of the Privy Council was set up with forty-two members on it, including the Duke of York, the archbishops of Canterbury and York, and the prime minister, to discuss the coronation plans. Later in the month Edward met the Duke of Norfolk, who as Earl Marshal would mastermind the event, to discuss plans. On the 20th, he again asked the Duke of York to chair another group, this time a coronation commission made up of representatives from the dominions as well as the UK.

At several points over the summer, the king met up with Cosmo Gordon Lang, the dour Scottish Archbishop of Canterbury. Lang had been close to George V but strongly disapproved of the new king's wayward lifestyle as Prince of Wales, later saying the company the prince kept was 'alien to all the best instincts and traditions of his people'. The archbishop was also fully aware of the king's determination to marry Mrs Simpson at all costs and agonised over whether he could administer the coronation oath to a man in a relationship with a divorced woman, given the Church's then rigid attitude to the dissolution of marriage.

For his part, the king couldn't stand the primate and was scathing about him in his memoirs, finding Lang to be 'rather … accustomed to the company of princes and statesmen, more interested in the pursuit of prestige and power than the abstractions of the human soul'. Elsewhere, he wrote that the archbishop had an 'over-anxiety to please' and, as the head of the Church, was 'almost too polished, too worldly'. When Lang mentioned George V questioning his heir's 'conduct', the king realised the man who was due to crown him was referring, admittedly obliquely, to Mrs Simpson: 'Wallis's name had of course not been mentioned but I knew that the Archbishop intended that I should know that she was the hidden burden of his discourse. He was clearly against our continued relationship.'

Putting the thorny issue of Mrs Simpson to one side, Lang was, according to his chaplain Alan Don, relieved that the king was positive about the sort of service his coronation would be and was prepared to follow the ritual laid down at the coronations of his father and grandfather, both of which he had attended. The archbishop had 'feared that he might want to cut out some of the more ancient and picturesque features'. Having said that, he was in agreement with the king's wish to omit the sermon and litany.

Lang, who went on to have a much better relationship with George VI and Queen Elizabeth, later claimed he was struck by how the king urged the Duke of York to follow the book of service while taking little interest himself. 'I wonder,' mused Lang, 'whether even then he had in the back of his mind some thought that the coronation might not be his but his brother's.'

While these weighty matters were being considered behind palace walls, the newspapers were drip, drip, dripping coronation updates to their readers. At the end of July, it was reported that the king had approved his picture and cypher on the coronation mugs that would be handed out to schoolchildren throughout the country as a souvenir. In mid-August, the palace also said the king had agreed to a lengthy return journey for his coronation procession, which was good news for those arranging seating along the route. Letters to newspaper editors complained about 'wild profiteering' and the 'prohibitively expensive' seat prices being suggested, so extending the route around Piccadilly Circus and Marble Arch would allow for far more vantage points from buildings as well as from temporary stands.

On 20 August, it was announced that a 32-page official souvenir programme would be made available featuring a message from the king plus a new photograph of him, a full text of the service and an introduction from the archbishop.

In October, Hendon Borough Council let it be known that a 21-acre site next to the North Circular Road, on what used to be the old sewage disposal works, was to be named the King Edward VIII Playing Fields as a permanent reminder of his coronation.

Before his short reign came to an end, Edward attended the State Opening of Parliament on 3 November. As he mentions in his memoirs, 'in pomp and pageantry it is second only to the Coronation', and he recalled, 'my nerves were taut', even though he was amused by 'an almost suffocating smell of mothballs given off by the colourful robes' of the peers seated before him. Usually it is the only occasion in the royal year when a monarch wears a crown but, as the Duke of Windsor recalled:

> because I had not been crowned yet [I] was required by custom to be covered during the reading of the 'Most Gracious Speech.' I decided to wear in place of the massive bejewelled headgear of kingship, the cocked hat that went with the uniform of an Admiral of the Fleet.

As it was his first appearance before parliament, he had to make a Declaration of Faith: 'I Edward VIII, do solemnly and sincerely in the presence of God profess, testify and declare that I am a faithful Protestant and that I will therefore uphold and maintain the said enactments to the best of my powers according to the law.' Had the coronation occurred before the State Opening of Parliament, Edward would have been obliged to say these words before being crowned. In his memoirs, Edward gives a clear indication of his feelings for such a tradition: 'I was brought up in the Protestant faith, yet the duty of uttering this outmoded sentiment was repugnant to me.' It is clear from this comment just how at odds his attitude was to the formalities of what amounted to a rehearsal for the coronation.

The king had one final minor duty to perform relating to his coronation. On Wednesday 2 December, he inspected the blue 'walking-out' uniform that the regular and territorial soldiers would wear at the coronation. After the event at Buckingham Palace, an army spokesman said, 'He suggested minor alterations which will be made before the general issue.' This came the morning after he had seen the prime minister

Stanley Baldwin, who told him that none of his governments in the UK or the empire would agree to a morganatic marriage to Mrs Simpson, so he had really only three choices: to give up his relationship with Wallis; to marry against the advice of his ministers who would then resign; or to abdicate. The same day the tiny report about Edward reviewing the troops in their uniforms was made, the newspapers were more concerned with the explosive story about his relationship with Wallis, which was now making headlines heralding the gravest constitutional crisis to affect the monarchy in the twentieth century.

GEORGE VI
1936–1952

As the spare rather than the heir, George had been allowed to serve in the Royal Navy and was present at the Battle of Jutland in the First World War. Had he been the firstborn, he may have been encouraged to marry a European princess, but instead was allowed to marry a commoner, albeit the daughter of an earl, Lady Elizabeth Bowes-Lyon. He is best remembered for sharing the hardships of his people during the Second World War with constant morale-boosting visits to bombed-out towns and cities. He died of a coronary thrombosis, while suffering from cancer, at the age of only 56.

Coronation of George VI, 12 May 1937

When Edward VIII abdicated in December 1936 to marry the twice-divorced American socialite Wallis Simpson, preparations were already well in hand for his coronation the following May. His brother and successor, George VI, decided not to postpone the ceremony, joking 'same date, but different king!'

It would make history as the first coronation to be broadcast live, though only in sound; the first to be filmed inside Westminster Abbey on newsreel film; and the first to have the procession filmed live on television in the BBC's first true outside broadcast. Having said all that, it was certainly not the first coronation to be littered with mishaps.

King George was born on 14 December 1895. By unlucky coincidence, this was the anniversary of the death of the prince consort, so there was really no option but to call the baby Albert to mollify the widowed Queen Victoria, who liked to spend the day in morbid introspection. 'Bertie', as he was known, attended the coronation of his grandfather Edward, another 'Bertie', King Edward VII. The 6-year-old prince, dressed in a Balmoral tartan kilt, fidgeted throughout apart from when his father, later George V, paid homage to the king.

George VI's coronation cost £454,000, more than three times the amount of King George's 1911 ceremony. George and his consort, Queen Elizabeth, acceded as the Emperor and Empress of India. Troops from the subcontinent, and every other nation the couple ruled over, took part in the procession. Some of the cost was for the construction of stands along the processional route, which for the return journey from the abbey to the palace stretched for nearly 6 miles (10km) through the capital.

Capturing the scene was the BBC's outside broadcast unit, which pushed the boat out by deploying three cameras – half its total number – to record the procession as it neared Apsley Gate at Hyde Park Corner. Queen Elizabeth pointed them out to the king, who smiled broadly as the Gold State Coach passed the BBC's chaps and their control van. The *Daily Mail* thought this telly lark might just take off: 'When the King and Queen appeared the picture was so vivid that one felt that this magical television is going to be one of the greatest of all modern inventions.'

There would be no live television from inside the abbey. The coverage then only reached 25 miles (40km) from central London, so the Archbishop of Canterbury, Cosmo Lang, deemed it 'not worthwhile'. There was also, he said, 'no possibility of censoring' live material. Instead, newsreel cameras captured the scene, which would eventually be shown at cinemas throughout the empire, once the archbishop and the Earl Marshal, the Duke of Norfolk, had sat through the entire recording and passed it for broadcast. In the event, they only asked for one moment – when Queen Mary wiped away a tear – to be omitted.

Another reason for their reluctance to admit live television was because the king suffered from a stammer, when his jaw could often be seen to tremor. Lang insensitively told the whole nation about this in a radio address two days after the abdication: 'When his people listen to him, they will note an occasional and momentary hesitation in his speech. But he has brought it under full control and to those who hear it, it need cause no sort of embarrassment, for it causes none for him who speaks' – or at least it hadn't until the meddling primate had opened his own mouth. It must therefore have been a delight for the king to tell the BBC's managing director, Lord Reith, that at the coronation rehearsal Lang and the dean kept colliding with each other and tripping up.

Victoria had been woken at 4 a.m. on her coronation day by the guns in Hyde Park. History repeated itself and George was woken at 3 a.m., also at Buckingham Palace, by the testing of loudspeakers, which, he wrote, 'might have been in our room'.

Two hours later it was the noise of bandsmen and troops marching past the palace that made sleep impossible.

George couldn't face eating breakfast and had a 'sinking feeling' thanks to what seemed an interminable wait until they could leave in the Gold State Coach at 10.43 a.m. One thing that did improve, though, was the weather, with a ray of sunshine following the morning rain at 11 a.m., as the royal couple arrived at the abbey.

From then on there was a catalogue of mini-disasters, most of them noted by the king in his journal account of the day. It began when a Presbyterian chaplain in the queen's procession fainted and no one seemed to know what to do with him.

When the king's procession set off from the Great West Door, he felt himself buffeted by the Bishop of Bath and Wells, who moved awkwardly, and the Bishop of Durham, who George thought 'fidgety'.

The same two clerics escorted George to the High Altar, where they messed things up again by both losing their places in the written order of service. Lang tilted his own copy down for the king to read only for George to discover, 'horror of horrors his thumb covered the words of the Oath'.

The Duke of Portland, carrying the queen's crown, and the Marquess of Salisbury, carrying the king's, both got their Order of the Garter collars caught up in the tasselled cushions they held.

To make sure the solid gold St Edward's Crown was put on the king the right way round, a tiny piece of red thread was attached beneath one of the prominent jewels at the front. When the dean collected it from the altar to bring it to Lang, he noticed it had gone. George believed 'some officious person must have removed it' and admitted he was never sure if he was crowned with it the right way round or back to front. The dean, William Foxley Norris, who died four months later, also fell down the steps carrying the weighty crown, which was fortunately attached to the cushion with ribbons. The unimpressed Duke of Somerset complained that the dean was like a 'half-awake bat, bewildered and incompetent, slow in all his actions'.

Finally, as the newly crowned monarch rose from St Edward's Chair, one of the two clumsy bishops stood on the royal robe and George had to tell him to get off it 'pretty sharply as I nearly fell down'.

Despite bedlam amongst the clergy, George found the service a deeply spiritual occasion and later wrote to Lang that 'I felt I was being helped all the time by Someone Else as you said I would'. The former prime minister, Ramsay MacDonald, recalled George telling him that 'for long periods at the Coronation ceremony he was unaware of what was happening'.

Someone who was aware was the 11-year-old heiress presumptive, Princess Elizabeth, who wrote in her own account of the day: 'I thought it all very, very wonderful and I expect the Abbey did, too. The arches and beams at the top were covered with a sort of haze of wonder as Papa was crowned, at least I thought so.' More prosaically, she and 6 year old Princess Margaret helped themselves to 'sandwiches, stuffed rolls, orangeade, and lemonade' in the abbey annexe. Back at Buckingham Palace, the princess wrote, 'we all went to the Balcony where millions of people were waiting below'. As the crowd shouted, 'we want the king' one time too many, George joked, 'the King wants his dinner.'

Before he could eat, history was to be made one final time that day when George became the first British monarch to broadcast to his people after the coronation. Speaking directly to them 'in their own homes' and 'with a full heart', he told them 'the Queen and I will always keep in our hearts the inspiration of this day'.

ELIZABETH II
1952–2022

Elizabeth II was queen regnant of thirty-two sovereign states during her lifetime and was head of state of fifteen nations at the time of her death, including Canada, Australia and New Zealand, as well as the UK. At the time of her accession she was 25, the same age Elizabeth I was when she became queen. She was the most travelled monarch in British history, the first to celebrate a Platinum Jubilee and a platinum wedding anniversary, the longest-lived UK monarch and the longest-reigning monarch, ruling for 70 years and 214 days.

Coronation of Elizabeth II, 2 June 1953

At the age of 27, Elizabeth II became the sixth queen regnant to be crowned at Westminster Abbey.

Preparations for the queen's coronation began in April 1952, two months after her accession and fourteen months before the ceremony on 2 June 1953. That particular day in early June was recommended by meteorologists as statistically it had the best chance of having sunny weather. Ironically, on the day the heavens opened.

The Duke of Edinburgh chaired the coronation commission at the suggestion of a member of the royal household, who told the prime minister, Winston Churchill, that Philip 'is insupportable when idle' and that the position would give him a meaningful role.

Unlike queen consorts, Prince Philip was not crowned and his role on the day was confined to accompanying his

Looking happy and glorious, and definitely relieved, the newly crowned Elizabeth II arrives back at Buckingham Palace following the ceremony. The camera flash lights up the golden orb and the Cullinan diamond in the sceptre, and even the royal footman can't resist a smile. (The Print Collector/Alamy Stock Photo)

wife to and from the abbey, being the first layman after the Archbishop of Canterbury to kneel before her to pay homage after she had been crowned. The queen also insisted that he should be by her side for Holy Communion.

Philip was instrumental in supporting the idea of a live television broadcast of the service. The queen was initially reluctant, and Churchill feared it would put unnecessary pressure on her, but after several opinion polls showed an overwhelming number of people supported the idea, the queen agreed, and 27 million people in the UK (out of the 36 million population) watched the ceremony on television, while 11 million listened on the radio. The anointing was the only part of the service the queen wouldn't allow to be televised. She was anointed with holy oil on the palms of her hands, her forehead and, unlike Victoria, on the breast.

On the morning of the coronation, her dresser and former nursery maid, Margaret 'Bobo' MacDonald, and her assistants helped the queen into her coronation dress, designed by Norman Hartnell. The queen asked the designer to make a gown of white satin that should conform to the line of her wedding dress. She also asked for floral emblems for all the Commonwealth nations besides the four UK national emblems Hartnell had shown her.

The queen and her six maids of honour attended two rehearsals at the abbey and also practised at Buckingham Palace with a sheet tied to her in place of the velvet train.

Since 1943, cosmetic advice had been given to the queen by Thelma Holland, who was the daughter-in-law of Oscar Wilde, having married his younger son Vyvyan. It is often presumed Mrs Holland did the make-up for the coronation, but on the day, Elizabeth chose to do her own. Her hair was styled by Henri Joerin, the royal hairdresser from 1939 to 1969.

The coronation bouquet was completely white and emblematic, made up of orchids and lilies-of-the-valley from England, stephanotis from Scotland, orchids from Wales and carnations from Northern Ireland and the Isle of Man.

One of her attendants said, 'You must be feeling nervous, Ma'am.' To which the equine-loving monarch replied, 'Yes but I really do think Aureole will win' – a reference to her runner in the Epsom Derby, to take place four days later. In the event, Aureole came second, the closest she ever came to winning this classic race.

She journeyed to the abbey with Prince Philip in the Gold State Coach, pulled by eight grey geldings, one of whom was named 'Eisenhower', after the Supreme Allied Commander during the Second World War. The queen later recalled the journey in the 4-ton coach as 'horrible' and 'not very comfortable', while the coach was 'not meant for travelling in at all'.

At the abbey, the queen was met by her maids of honour and the Mistress of the Robes, the Dowager Duchess of Devonshire. As they took up the satin handles on either side of the 18ft-long (5.4m) train, the queen said, 'Ready, girls?' and they moved off.

The coronation service took almost three hours – Victoria's lasted five – beginning at 11.15 a.m. and ending when the queen left at 2 p.m. During the service, the queen used three different chairs: the Chair of Estate, which was in front of the Royal Gallery (and is now on display at Buckingham Palace); she then moved to the carved oak Coronation Chair, first used at the coronation of Edward II in 1308; and then, finally, to the gilt wood Throne Chair (which today is kept in the state apartments at Windsor Castle).

Elizabeth was crowned with the solid gold St Edward's Crown and, like her father and grandfather before her, would only wear it on the day of the coronation. For the return journey to Buckingham Palace, the queen wore the lighter Imperial State Crown.

Four-and-a-half-year-old Prince Charles was brought into the abbey to witness the moment of crowning, sitting between the Queen Mother and Princess Margaret. He said, 'Look, it's Mummy!' and the queen gave him a smile.

Also in the Royal Gallery on the south side of the High Altar were Philip's three surviving sisters, Margarita, Theodora and Sophie. They had lobbied hard to be included in the guest list, having been excluded from the wedding in 1947. Having all been married to German aristocrats, it was deemed too soon after the Second World War for them to attend the nuptials. They were permitted to attend with their husbands, but with just two of their children each and no other German relations. Also banned was the Duke of Windsor, at the suggestion of Elizabeth. According to Archbishop Fisher, 'The Queen would be less willing than anyone to have him there.' A former monarch witnessing the anointing of a new one just didn't sit well.

Overseas VIPs who did attend were later given coronation chicken at a buffet lunch following the ceremony. It was created by the florist Constance Spry, who suggested a recipe of cold chicken in a cream curry sauce with an accompanying salad of rice, green peas and mixed herbs.

The official coronation photos were taken at Buckingham Palace by Cecil Beaton. Philip would have liked his close friend Baron Nahum to take the official photographs, but the Queen Mother lobbied for, and succeeded in getting, Beaton. Anne Glenconner, then Lady Anne Coke, one of the maids of honour, recalled, 'Cecil Beaton was in a stew, hopping up and down, and … the Duke of Edinburgh – he was an amateur photographer – kept on saying, "no you've got to be there". Tired of Philip arranging the group, 'in the end Cecil Beaton said, "Look I'm taking the photographs you know, I think I'd better get on with it".

Speaking of her coronation, the queen said in a 2018 BBC documentary:

It's the beginning of one's life really as a sovereign.

It is sort of a pageant of chivalry and an old-fashioned way of doing things. I've seen one coronation and been the recipient in the other, which is pretty remarkable.

BIBLIOGRAPHY

Akrigg, G.P.V., *Jacobean Pageant: Or the Court of King James I* (Atheneum, 1978)

Alice, Princess, Countess of Athlone, *For My Grandchildren: Some Reminiscences of Her Royal Highness Princess Alice, Countess of Athlone* (Evans Brothers Limited, 1966)

Allmand, Christopher, *Henry V* (University of California Press, 1992)

Ashley, Maurice, *James II* (J.M. Dent & Sons, 1977)

Ashley, Maurice, *The Life and Times of King John* (Weidenfeld & Nicolson, 1972)

Barlow, Frank, *William Rufus* (Second Edition) (Yale University Press, 2000)

Baxter, Stephen, *William III* (Longman, 1966)

Binski, Paul, *Westminster Abbey and the Plantagenets* (Yale, 1995)

Borman, Tracy, *Matilda: Wife of the Conqueror, First Queen of England* (Vintage, 2012)

Bradford, Sarah, *George VI: The Dutiful King* (Penguin, 2011)

Brett, Martin, *The English Church Under Henry I* (Oxford University Press, 1975)

Brooke, John, *King George III* (Constable, 1972)

Carpenter, David, *The Minority of Henry III* (Methuen, 1990)

Chancellor, John, *The Life and Times of Edward I* (Weidenfeld & Nicolson, 1981)

Chapman, Hester, *The Last Tudor King: A Study of Edward VI* (Macmillan, 1958)

Chrimes, S.B., *Henry VII* (Yale University Press, 1999)

Cook, Petronella, *Queen Consorts of England: The Power Behind the Throne* (Facts on File, 1993)

Crawford, Anne, *The Yorkists: The History of a Dynasty* (Hambledon Continuum, 2007)

Crouch, David, *The Normans: The History of a Dynasty* (Hambledon, Continuum 2002)

Curtis, Gila, *The Life and Times of Queen Anne* (Weidenfeld & Nicolson, 1972)

Davis, R.H.C., *King Stephen 1135–1154* (Third Edition) (Longman, 1990)

Dockray, Keith, *Henry V* (Tempus Publishing, 2004)

Dockray, Keith, *Richard III: A Reader in History* (Alan Sutton, 1988)

Douglas, David C., *William the Conqueror: The Norman Impact Upon England* (Eyre & Spottiswoode, 1964)

Falkus, Gila, *The Life and Times of Edward IV* (Weidenfeld & Nicolson, 1981)

Freeman, Edward A., *The Reign of William Rufus and the Accession of Henry the First* (Clarendon Press, 1882)

Garmonsway, G.N., *The Anglo-Saxon Chronicle* (Revised Edition) (J.M. Dent & Sons, 1960)

Giles. J.A. (trans.), *Roger of Wendover's Flowers of History* (Henry G. Bohn, 1849)

Given-Wilson, Chris, *Henry IV* (Yale University Press, 2016)

Green, David, *Queen Anne* (HarperCollins, 1970)

Green, Judith, *The Government of England Under Henry I* (Cambridge University Press, 1989)

Gregg, Edward, *Queen Anne* (Ark Paperbacks, 1984)

Gregg, Pauline, *King Charles I* (J.M. Dent & Sons, 1981)

Hallam, Elizabeth (ed.), *The Plantagenet Chronicles* (Weidenfeld & Nicolson, 1986)

Hervey, John, Lord, *Memoirs of the Reign of George II: Vol. 1* (John Murray, 1848)

Hibbert, Christopher, *Charles I* (Harper & Row, 1968)

Hibbert, Christopher, *George IV: Regent and King* (Allen Lane, 1973)

Hicks, Michael, *The Prince in the Tower* (Tempus Publishing, 2007)

Hobsbawm, Eric and Ranger, Terence, *The Invention of Tradition* (Cambridge University Press, 1983)

Holmes, Frederick, *The Sickly Stuarts: The Medical Downfall of a Dynasty* (Sutton Publishing, 2003)

Howell, Margaret, *Eleanor of Provence* (Blackwell, 1998)

Hutchison, Harold, *Edward II: 1284–1327* (Barnes & Noble, 1971)

Hutton, Ronald, *Charles II: King of England, Scotland and Ireland* (Clarendon Press, 1989)

Jenks, Edward, *Edward Plantagenet* (G.P. Putnam's Sons, 1902)

Johnson, Paul, *The Life and Times of Edward III* (Weidenfeld & Nicolson, 1973)

Jordan, W.K., *Edward VI: The Young King* (Allen & Unwin, 1968)

Judd, Denis, *The Life and Times of George V* (Weidenfeld & Nicolson, 1973)

Keay, Anna, *The Crown Jewels: Official Guidebook* (Historic Royal Palaces, 2002)

Latham, Robert (ed.), *Pepys' Diary* (Guild Publishing, 1981)

Lee, Sir Sidney, *King Edward VII: A Biography, Vol II. The Reign* (Macmillan & Co. Ltd, 1927)

Loades, David, *Mary Tudor: A Life* (Basil Blackwell, 1989)

Longford, Elizabeth, *Victoria R.I.* (Weidenfeld & Nicolson, 1964)

Marie Louise, Her Highness Princess, *My Memories of Six Reigns* (Evans Brothers Limited, 1956)

Mason, Emma, *King Rufus: The Life & Murder of William II of England* (The History Press, 2008)

Maxwell, Sir Herbert (ed.), *The Chronicle of Lanercost: 1272–1346* (Glasgow University Press, 1913)

Miller, John, *The Life and Times of William and Mary* (Weidenfeld & Nicolson, 1974)

Morris, Christopher (ed.), *The Journeys of Celia Fiennes* (The Cresset Press, 1947)

Morris, Marc, *A Great and Terrible King: Edward I and the Forging of Britain* (Pegasus Books, 2015)

Mortimer, Ian, *The Fears of Henry IV* (Vintage Books, 2008)

Mortimer, Ian, *The Perfect King: The Life of Edward III, Father of the English Nation* (Vintage, 2008)

Neale, J.E., *Queen Elizabeth* (Jonathan Cape, 1934)

Nicolson, Harold, *King George V* (Constable, 1952)

Ormrod, W.M., *The Reign of Edward III* (Tempus Publishing, 2000)

Packe, Michael, *King Edward III* (Ark Paperbacks, 1983)

Prestwich, Michael, *Edward I* (Yale University Press, 1997)

Ridley, Jane, *Bertie: A Life of Edward VII* (Chatto & Windus, 2012)

Ridley, Jane, *George V: Never a Dull Moment* (Chatto & Windus, 2021)

Ridley, Jasper, *The Life and Times of Mary Tudor* (Weidenfeld & Nicolson, 1973)

Robb, Nesca, *William of Orange: A Personal History* (Heinemann, 1966)

Roberts, Andrew, *George III: The Life and Reign of Britain's Most Misunderstood Monarch* (Allen Lane, 2021)

Rodwell, Warwick, *The Coronation Chair and Stone of Scone: History, Archaeology and Conservation* (Oxbow Books, 2013)

Ross, Charles, *Edward IV* (University of California Press, 1974)

Ross, Charles, *Richard III* (Methuen, 1981)

Salzman, L.F., *Edward I* (Constable, 1968)

Saul, Nigel, *Richard II* (Yale University Press, 1997)

Senior, Michael, *The Life and Times of Richard II* (Weidenfeld & Nicolson, 1981)

Somerset, Anne, *Queen Anne: The Politics of Passion* (Knopf, 2013)

Speck, W.A., *James II* (Routledge, 2013)

Starkey, David, *Six Wives: The Queens of Henry VIII* (Chatto & Windus, 2003)

Stewart, Alan, *Cradle King: The Life of James VI & I* (Chatto & Windus, 2003)

Strong, Roy, *Coronation: A History of Kingship and the British Monarchy* (HarperCollins, 2005)

Styles, Dorothy & Allmand, C.T., 'The Coronations of Henry VI', *History Today*, Vol. 32, Issue 5, May 1982

Sutton, Anne & Hammond, P.W. (eds), *The Coronation of Richard III: The Extant Documents* (Sutton Publishing, 1983)

Trench, Charles, *George II* (Allen Lane, 1973)

Van der Kiste, John, *William and Mary* (Sutton Publishing, 2003)

Walters, John, *The Royal Griffin: Frederick Prince of Wales, 1707–51* (Jarrolds, 1972)

Warren, W.L., *Henry II* (University of California Press, 1973)

Warren, W.L., *King John* (W.W. Norton & Company, 1961)

Weir, Alison, *Elizabeth of York: The First Tudor Queen* (Jonathan Cape, 2013)

Weir, Alison, *Henry VIII: King and Court* (Vintage, 2008)

Weir, Alison, *Isabella: She-Wolf of France, Queen of England* (Vintage Books, 2012)

Whitelock, Anna, *Mary Tudor: England's First Queen* (Bloomsbury, 2009)

Williams, Neville, *The Life and Times of Elizabeth I* (Weidenfeld & Nicolson, 1972)

Williams, Neville, *The Life and Times of Henry VII* (Weidenfeld & Nicolson, 1973)

Windsor, Duke of, *A King's Story* (Cassell & Co., 1951)

Wordsworth, Christopher, *The Manner of the Coronation of King Charles the First of England at Westminster, 2 Feb. 1626* (Henry Bradshaw Society, 1892)

Wylie, James H., *The Reign of Henry V: Vol. 1* (Cambridge University Press, 1914)

Ziegler, Philip, *King Edward VIII: The Official Biography* (Collins, 1990)

Websites

www.thegazette.co.uk/London/issue

www.nationalarchives.gov.uk/education/resources/richard-ii/attendance-at-richards-coronation-1377

www.westminster-abbey.org/about-the-abbey/history/royalty

You may also enjoy ...

978 1 80399 281 5

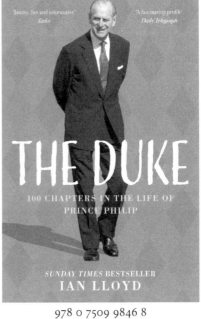

978 0 7509 9846 8